Diaries of an Egyptian Princess

Nevine Abbas Halim

First Edition
1000 copies

© 2009 Nevine Abbas Halim

© 2009 Zeitouna
30 Abdine Square, Cairo, Egypt 11111
admin@zeitouna.com

ISBN 977 5864 23 2
Dar el-Kutub 21445/09

Printed in Egypt

Diaries of an Egyptian Princess

Nevine Abbas Halim

Zeitouna
Cairo

Mohamed Ali Pasha the Great

Khedive Ismail, son of Ibrahim Pasha, son of Mohamed Ali Pasha

Halim Pasha, son of Mohamed Ali Pasha

Princess Tawhida, daughter of Khedive Ismail and wife of Mansour Pasha Yeghen

Princess Pakise, wife of Prince Osman Fazil

Wahida, daughter of Princess Tawhida and wife of Ahmed Midhat Yeghen Pasha

Princess Ulfette, daughter of Prince Osman Fazil and wife of Prince Ibrahim Halim

Ahmed Midhat Yeghen Pasha

Prince Ibrahim Halim, son of Halim Pasha, son of Mohamed Ali Pasha

Princess Tawhida Halim, daughter of Wahida and Ahmed Midhat Yeghen Pasha

Prince Abbas Halim, son of Prince Ibrahim Halim, son of Halim Pasha

Nevine, Mohamed Ali and Ulvia Abbas Halim

Left: King Fouad I, son of Khedive Ismail
Above: Princess Fawzia, Prince Farouk and Princess Faiza, children of King Fouad

Palais. d'Abdine   Le 6 Juillet 1930.

Monseigneur,

    J'ai eu l'honneur de soumettre à Sa Majesté le Roi, notre Auguste Souverain, la lettre de Votre Seigneurie en date du 2 Juillet.

    Notre Auguste Souverain, s'est réjoui d'apprendre la naissance d'une fille à Votre Seigneurie, et m'ordonne de Vous transmettre des félicitations.

    En m'acquittant de cet agréable devoir, je prie Votre Seigneurie d'agréer l'expression de mes respectueux hommages.

Le Grand Chambellan

I was born on June 30th, 1930 in Alexandria. This noteworthy event occurred in the house of my paternal grandfather. Afterwards, it was sold and promptly pulled down. My sister Ulvia Ulfette and my brother Mohamed Ali were born in Mummy's house in Garden City. Her father had given her the house before her first marriage. From that marriage she had a son, Ismaïl, ten years older than me. For some unsound reason, he was always called Totes.

As my father's first born, even though a girl, I was greeted with great excitement. My father was delighted with me and Mummy was always happy with whatever pleased him.

Both my parents were descended from Mohamed Ali Pasha, the founder of modern Egypt who pulled the country out of the Middle Ages.

Egypt was part of the Ottoman Empire. Mohamed Ali's son, Ibrahim Pasha, a brilliant general like his father, took Greater Syria when the Ottoman Sultan reneged on his promise to grant it to Mohamed Ali as his reward for quelling a rebellion in Greece. The Great Powers of the time, France and Great Britain took fright and obliged Mohamed Ali to withdraw and accept only the hereditary title of Viceroy of Egypt and possession of the Sudan.

In 1914, Egypt – still nominally a part of the Ottoman Empire – was occupied by the British. They removed Khedive Abbas Hilmi II from the throne as he was loyal to the Ottomans and installed Prince Hussein Kamel as Sultan. When he died in 1917, his brother, Fouad took his place. In 1922, when Great Britain finally agreed to acknowledge Egypt as an independent state, Fouad took the title of king and the country was declared a constitutional monarchy.

My father returned to Egypt after the First World War; having fought on the Ottoman–German side, the British would not allow him back until 1920. We'll leave him for the moment and turn to my mother.

***

Nevine with Prince Abbas Halim and Princess Tawhida

My mother, Tawhida Yeghen, the only child of Ahmed Midhat Yeghen Pasha and Wahida Yeghen was born on April 11, 1901. The Yeghens were Mohamed Ali's nephews who joined their uncle in Egypt when he became viceroy. On her mother's side, she was descended from Khedive Ismaïl by his daughter, Tawhida, for whom she was named.

Princess Tawhida was thoroughly spoilt. She insisted on marrying a relative, Mansour Yeghen Pasha. She and her sister had been trying their hands at poetry, which they submitted for criticism to Mansour Pasha, a known connoisseur. She fell in love with the man of the "admirably-worded phrases" and her affections were returned.

The Khedive had nothing against Mansour Pasha but found them unsuited. Princess Tawhida insisted, but her father had been right. Too proud to admit her mistake, she did her best to be a good wife. She was a terrible spendthrift and after her early death, her husband locked himself up in his country estate for seven years until he had settled all her debts.

Princess Tawhida had three daughters and a son who died young. Her youngest daughter Wahida was my grandmother, whom we never knew because she died when Mummy was ten.

***

My mother's 1918 diary gives a picture of her life. She was seventeen years old and the "terrible" First World War was not yet over. Her father had just been named Governor of Alexandria.

She was a very busy girl with an English governess, a French teacher, Italian violin and piano teachers and another Frenchwoman who gave her painting lessons. Each teacher wanted their "homework" done first, the poor child had to rise at 5.30 in the morning to practice the piano. When she was a small child,

25

My mother, Tawhida Yeghen

she fared worse, as she had Fraülein all morning and French, Turkish and Arabic lessons all afternoon at her cousins' house in Daher just outside Cairo. The teachers were very strict and she was always being punished for staring out of the window or not sitting up straight. Her pigtail was often tied to the back of her chair.

She'd been born with something wrong with her right hip. Her parents took her to specialists in Paris, Berlin and Munich, finally deciding on Professor Lorenz in Vienna. The operation was performed when she was five and was successful, but she had to keep her right leg in Plaster of Paris for eight months. Afterwards, she could walk for several miles and play squash and tennis with an almost imperceptible limp. When she was older, the limp became worse, the good leg compensating for the bad one. And what with arthritis, she was in almost continual pain and walking became more and more of an effort. But Mummy was a fighter, getting dressed was really bad at times, but she did it then walked to the bar for her two Dry Martinis and salmon sandwich lunch.

I'm getting ahead of myself. Grandpa was Governor of Alexandria and had to rent a house as it did not come with the job. Alexandrians did not rent their houses for long periods, so every few months, Mummy and Grandpa had to move. She hated this upheaval and the general disorder it produced.

Grandpa later became Minister of Agriculture and then Minister of Foreign Affairs. He was one of the founders of the Banque Misr and its first chairman. He was also President of the Khedivial Mail Line. He was either very modest or very retiring, but certainly very strict. Mummy said he'd been so gay and lively but he'd had a slight stroke when we were very young and had never fully recovered. We never saw that side, he was rather cool and distant with us. His nieces, Aunts Shahira and Malek, would pay him visits and kiss his hand. He then told me that I had to kiss his hand and I refused, saying I had no intention of kissing a man's hand. This was very brave of me, I might add.

Not long ago, I saw him on French TV standing with a group of other luminaries at the entrance of Tutankhamen's tomb upon its discovery in 1922 by Mr. Carter. He had a very naughty smile.

Mummy was born at Incha Palace in Cairo, which later became the Ministry of War. She described it as "a hideous though darkly impressive place of roughly 300 rooms" belonging to Mansour Pasha. By the time he had paid all Princess Tawhida's debts, he had become very miserly and life was pretty spartan for poor Mummy.

In 1908, Grandpa moved to a house in Abbassia, outside Cairo and bought a motorcar. He was always very avant-garde. When his wife Wahida died in 1911, they moved again to the middle of town. One of his friends, Mr. Hooker, knowing that Grandpa was looking for a governess for his daughter, proposed a Miss Kate Matthews. She and Mummy were to become devoted friends. "She taught me to live and molded my character…she had travelled widely and had that international outlook that made her such a delightful person."

In Cairo, they moved to a house in Garden City. Rumour had it that Grandpa won it gambling. He was a terrific gambler and lost and won fortunes. Thankfully he won the last time around. He stopped gambling in Egypt when one morning returning from an all-night session, his daughter saw him tired and dishevelled and he swore never to risk that again.

Although he adored his daughter, Grandpa was terribly severe as far as men were concerned. No man was allowed near her and she could not visit her girlfriends in case she met a male relative at their houses. As a child she did meet her first cousins, Mohamed and Abdallah Izzet with whom she had lessons. She saw Daddy once in Alexandria when he came to dinner. Another exception was her first cousin Ismaïl Daoud, who was married to Sultan Hussein's daughter, Princess Samiha. He taught Mummy to ride at Zaafaran Palace where his mother, Mum's Aunt Senieh, lived. Grandpa's severity was

My grandfather, Ahmed Midhat Yeghen Pasha

soon vindicated, as Ismaïl seems to have fallen in love with his little cousin. "Ismaïl came to see me for a few minutes. I was distinctly cold this time and pulled my hand away when I saw he was keeping it in his for some time."

But Mummy was a naughty girl. "There was a war on and Cairo and Alexandria were overflowing with good looking soldiers. The Australians used to exercise their horses around Garden City and I would hang out of the window to watch them go by, purposely loosening my long light-brown hair. The men on horseback would always look up at the windows and blow kisses and I would be thrilled at having done something so illicit."

In 1918, the Spanish flu was raging and his doctor advised Grandpa to send his daughter to Luxor with Kate. Mum loved the three weeks at the Winter Palace. Cousin Ismaïl and his wife were there and Mum went fox hunting in the fields around Luxor. She was given a huge English horse and she let it do as it pleased, jump walls and irrigation canals, with Ismaïl cantering behind yelling "Tatty, Tatty, hold your reins, for God's sake, hold your reins! Don't you remember what I taught you?" Mum didn't and couldn't have cared less and didn't fall off or cause any disturbance with her "unethical riding."

Kate Matthews had to fight Grandpa for every small entertainment, such as tea parties with her friends and games of tennis. But then the Armistice was signed and Kate, who was not well and terrified of the anti-British unrest in Cairo, went home to England. For Mummy, this was dreadful. To escape, she agreed to an arranged marriage. She was eighteen and Mohamed Assem was just twenty when they married on November 16, 1919.

At nineteen "I had a son, a little tow-headed baby that looked almost an albino." His name was Ismaïl, but was always called Totes. The marriage was a disaster with even more restrictions than under the paternal wing. Poor Totes suffered the most. Mummy had so disliked his father, it influenced her feelings towards him. She was a tough disciplinarian and Totes got the brunt of it. She

Prince Ismail Daoud

was not particularly loving to the rest of us. She'd been brought up the English way, no tears, no sloppy hugging and kissing. To this day, we don't cry in public and we take our medicine without a murmur. I still find it difficult to understand public displays of suffering or affection and even more difficult to watch the bereaved wailing in front of TV cameras. And no psychiatrist helped us get over the deaths of our loved ones.

One day Grandpa brought a lady to tea, Lady Evelyn Cobbold, who was to become a very dear friend. She was the daughter of the Earl of Dunmore and you'd better not forget it. She was recently divorced from Mr. Cobbold, who, horrors, was in "trade." In fact, I think he was a very successful banker. She "was spending a few weeks at the Mena House sunbathing for an injury sustained to her back from a fall. Although I was only twenty and I would have thought pretty boring for her, she took a great liking to me and invited me and my husband to spend a week at Glencarron Lodge in Scotland which she had just bought after divorcing her husband. She was going to have a very small house party of stalkers she wrote…My husband instantly got in touch with my father behind my back saying there would be men at Glencarron Lodge. We were in Brussels at the time and I got a severe letter of reprimand from my father. I remember crying with disappointment over my letter to Evelyn telling her why I could not accept her fascinating invitation. But Evelyn would not take no for an answer. She promptly wrote and said she would not include any other men—that my husband and I and an American woman would be her only guests. She was obviously and understandingly disgusted when I arrived and told her the procedure taken to stop my visit. I enjoyed every moment of my stay. The Lodge was still very primitive in those days, although she put in quite a few improvements since its purchase—only fireplaces, no central heating yet and it was pretty cold. Evelyn told me what clothes to get in London and I felt fine, but the poor old American woman

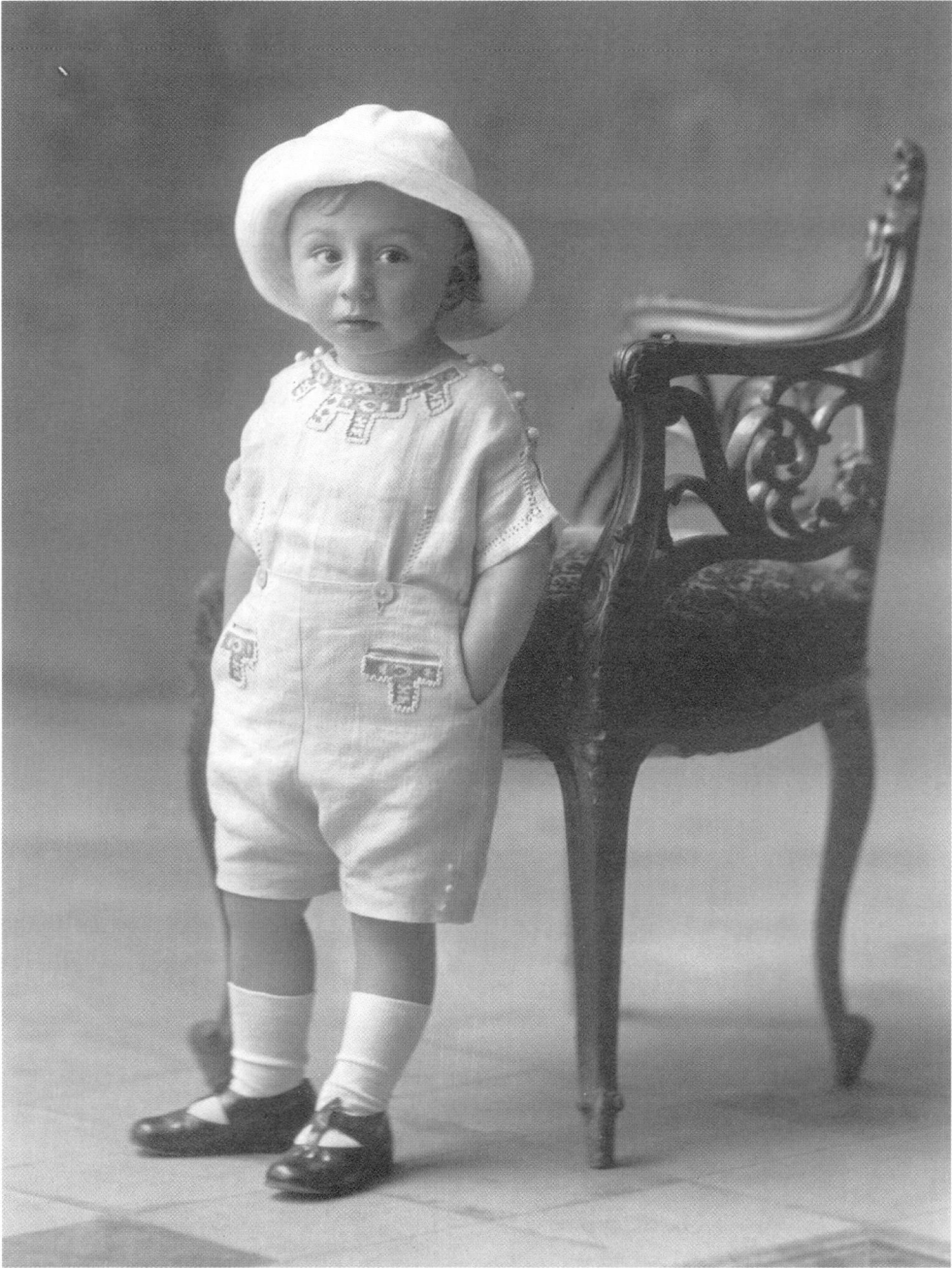

Ismail Assem (Totes)

wore about six woollies under her fur coat in the house and kept up a continual dirge about freezing to death. My husband was sent stalking with Grant, the then Head Stalker, and wounded a deer which Grant was fortunately able to finish off. I went stalking with Evelyn once, she was a remarkable woman and could keep a pace over the hills that I was quite unable to follow despite my youth. We went for lovely drives…picnics in the heather, lunches and teas with her friends. One lunch stands out in my memory particularly, at Sir Arthur and Lady Murray's lovely house and especially the garden, of which Lady Murray was justifiably proud." While Lady Murray and Evelyn discussed plants, Sir Arthur took Mum into the house, having found out something of her background, he said: "I want to show you what an ancestor of yours gave my father." It was a sword given to him by Mohamed Ali Pasha, the conqueror of Egypt. Sir Arthur's father had been in Egypt and written an excellent biography of Mohamed Ali the Great, which the Pasha had greatly appreciated.

The following year, the Assems were again invited to Glencarron with no mention of the guest list. There were two men present to the great discomfort of Mr. Assem and Mum's secret amusement.

Life dragged on in utter boredom. "Girls were using make-up and cutting their hair. I was not allowed to do either and after several furious rows, I told my husband to get out." Grandpa had given the house her in 1914, so the rumour he'd won it at cards may have been wrong. Mummy told her father what she'd done who replied that if she had put up with that bore any longer, he'd have been disgusted. Mummy glared at him and reminded him that he was the one who had chosen the fellow. She was just twenty-two.

After the separation life became much more amusing. She saw a great deal of her cousin Emina Toussoun. "She was then Princess Omar Halim. Prince Omar had gone big game shooting and he kept open house to friends and

Princess Emine Toussoun, daughter of Prince Omar Toussoun

relatives. It was a lovely house and she enjoyed entertaining. Still no males were allowed. She gave a reception for our cousin Loutfia's wedding to Ahmed Hassanein, the explorer of the *Lost Oasis*. Loutfia's father, Seifullah Yousry Pasha, had been the first Egyptian Minister to Washington. Emina was able to get the British Air Force Band to play dance music for us, and we girls danced between ourselves to the wide eyed astonishment of the band…That was the way we still lived in 1926 in Egypt."

Grandpa loved France and had bought a small house in Brunoy "about 17 km south of Paris. There were 15 acres of grounds, the boundary on one part of the estuary Yerre and beyond the highway to Fontainebleau was the lovely forest of Sémart. In April 1926, we left by ship for Marseilles. Emina arranged to travel with us and we had a gay journey together. My father and his retinue of servants went by train to Brunoy." (Totes once described the retinue, consisting of several dogs, cats, birds, as well as Grandpa's housekeeper, ironer, valet and a mountain of luggage. Totes carefully avoided any close contact with this appalling assembly, pretending not to know them.)

Mummy and Aunt Emina "took three cars and chauffeurs, two Italians and one Englishman." The girls drove in Grandpa's Spider Lancia with a leaking canvas top in pouring rain, while two closed cars, Mummy's old Rolls driven by Olivarès and Aunt's new Isotta Fraschini driven by Alfredo followed.

Grandpa moved to Vittel, but thanks to Aunt Emina, Mum managed to go up to Paris several times a week and even went to her first nightclub, Le Perroquét, at the age of 25. "I loved these outings, it was my first taste of freedom. My divorce was still dragging and I intended to enjoy every minute of our stay in Europe. My father finally gave in to my pestering and took a huge apartment on Boulevard de Courcelles which meant being much more with Emina. I had a red sports Bugatti, which I drove myself. By this time Omar Halim had joined his wife, she had taken an apartment on Avenue Victor Hugo.

Prince Omar Halim, son of Prince Said Halim Pasha, son of Halim Pasha

Tawhida

Brunoy

My grandmother Princess Ulfette Fazil and her daughter, Aunt Bedia Halim

My mother Tawhida and her cousin Aicha Aziza, Princess Mohamed Ali Hassan

Omar played polo and we often went to Bagatelle to watch the matches. She and I were great tennis fans and followed the French International Championship with wild enthusiasm. Suzanne Lenglen, Tilden, Richards and the wonderful four Musketeers Cochet, Brugnon, Lacoste, Borotra."

The Omar Halims (he was Dad's first cousin) were a handsome pair, he with thick black eyebrows, which gave him a devilish look and Aunt Emina very attractive if not classically beautiful, tall with black hair tinged with blue and full of life and fun.

Mum met Dad at Roland Garros. She had not seen him since childhood and now saw a great deal of him. The Omar Halims were off to Deauville for the polo season and then to Biarritz where they had taken a house. Mum was stuck with Grandpa in Vittel, where he was supposedly taking the waters, but spent most of his time at the casino. He was a surprisingly lucky gambler.

Mummy drove to Vittel, utterly refusing to have anything to do with Grandpa and his zoo. She loved her Bugatti and while in Paris caused quite a sensation tearing up the Champs Elysées and the Avenue des Acacias in the Bois. In Vittel, however, she was terribly bored, so when Aunt Emina invited her to Biarritz, she pleaded with her father to let her go. She drove there via Paris and sent her enormous wardrobe trunk by rail directly to Aunt Emina's house. On arriving in Biarritz she found to her horror that a large bottle of red mouthwash had broken and utterly ruined all her dresses. Thankfully, Grandpa arrived shortly after and upon hearing his daughter's tale of woe, gave her sufficient funds to replace her clothes. This made sure that Mummy had a marvellous time in Biarritz.

"The Balsans lived...at one end of the grounds. Madame Balsan was Consuelo Vanderbilt, the former Duchess of Marlborough and they struck me as a wonderfully happy couple." Mr. Balsan had long been associated with Coco Chanel. Mum met the Michel de Zoghebs, she was the French actress

Tawhida in her red Bugatti, Paris 1926

Prince Abbas Halim and Princess Tawhida in Deauville

Gabrielle Dorziat of whom she grew very fond. She saw them again in Egypt. Emina had invited Prince and Princess Osman of Turkey to stay and "some days later Abbas Halim arrived from Deauville with two cars, his own Mercedes and a beaten up huge Renault whose owner had lost so much at the casino that he persuaded Abbas to accept it in lieu of cash. Between the Casino and the cabarets, dinner parties and dancing we seldom got to bed before 5 a.m. or later. Emina who shared her room with me (the house party had grown) would sleep late, but I would creep out to go bathing or play tennis. I didn't seem to need much sleep...I gave a dinner party at the Réserve at St. Jean de Luz. I remember it well as I chose Abbas to be host for me as we were both single. I was very sorry when I had to leave and go back to Paris, but the season was over and most of the party was also returning to Paris. About 10 days after arriving, I got a phone call from Abbas; he had made a detour to Cannes and said he had just arrived and would I lunch with him, he would drive me out to St. Germain-en-Laye and we could lunch at the Pavillon Henri IV."

Mum arranged to meet him at Claridge's as she was still very wary of her father. "It was a beautiful day and the Pavillon Henri IV is a lovely spot, especially when you are young and you feel the interest in you of the person you are with...and so the weeks rolled on, during one of our outings...I suggested he should marry a very pretty cousin of mine...His query was 'What's wrong with you?' 'Oh,' I said airily, 'I'm out of the question. I'm not divorced yet, it has already been three years. Also I'm in no hurry.'"

Back in Egypt, Mum got her divorce for £E 6,000 in cash. The person who arranged it was Dad, whom she eventually married on her birthday, April 11, 1928. Shortly after their marriage they sailed for Europe to attend the Olympic Games in Amsterdam. Dad was on the Olympic Committee and Egypt won the weight lifting championship and the Greco-Roman wrestling.

Before we leave Mummy, a few words on her son, Ismail/Totes. When his

Prince Abbas Halim

mother remarried, he entered a titled family and he had the misfortune of being born without one. This gave him a complex that drove us mad. He could be very sweet and great fun only to change suddenly to being sarcastic and critical. He loved us and hated us and wanted above all to be a nabil. He met the King in Rome after the revolution and asked him for a paper stating he was a nabil. The King kindly obliged, although Totes had no right to the title. The whole concept of royalty is birth. You have to be born a prince. His second marriage to Seldjouk, a Turkish Imperial Princess and former wife of Djezouly Ratib, somewhat calmed his craving for titles. Her mother was Princess Emine Halim, but he played that down.

* * *

My father was the great-grandson of Mohamed Ali Pasha by his youngest son, Halim Pasha. The Great Family Feud began with Halim Pasha and Dad's maternal great-grandfather, Prince Mustafa Fazil, when Ismail Pasha received the right of male primogeniture from the Sultan as opposed to the old system of the eldest male in the family inheriting the throne. It would have been Prince Fazil and then Halim Pasha's turns to reign. Ismail Pasha suspected them of plotting against him, sent them into exile and confiscated their property.

This rankled my father all his life. He had no money. His cousins, Mohamed Ali Ibrahim and Ismail Daoud inherited fortunes and were very generous, but Dad was a proud man and he blamed his father.

He is difficult to size up. He did not keep a diary. Although we found lots of notes, they are not really helpful in reading his thoughts. He is all in nuances, in some situations straightforward, in others a complete mystery. He'll never tell you what he really thinks of you, except on the rare occasion when he loses his temper. And even then, how sure are you that it was not

Prince Abbas Halim in German officer uniform

deliberate? We children loved him utterly, nothing he did or said could be anything but perfect. Of course, he was not the disciplinarian. That was Mum's task. She was jealous of our over-powering love for him, but only at times. She herself loved him so much that it was only much later that she resented the fact that we obviously, all four of us, Totes included, loved Daddy more than we loved her.

You could not NOT love Daddy. He could charm a snake off a tree, was kind to a fault, treated the doorman with the same courtesy as the King and was quite unable to refuse to help anybody in distress. He was also extremely good-looking, which as we all know is so helpful.

Daddy went to school and military academy in Germany and was in the prestigious Uhland regiment when the War broke out. This regiment was made up of foreign princes and aristocrats, as well as Germany's cream of the cream. The Kronprinz was the Commanding Officer I believe, because Dad told us that after a long night he was late for inspection and had thrown his greatcoat over his evening clothes and the Kronprinz had noticed at once. Dad fought in the War first in the German army and then in the Turkish air force. He was wounded twice, once in Russia seriously in his right arm. The army doctors managed to save it, but he could not bend it properly and when eating or lighting a cigarette, his arm stuck out awkwardly. Some silly snobs thought it was a new affectation and imitated him to his unholy amusement.

He was born in 1897 in Alexandria when Egypt was part of the Ottoman Empire. We still have his Ottoman passport. He also had the title of "prince", as did all the immediate members of the Royal Family. He was not an Imperial prince, but an Egyptian one. People get mixed up about this, because there was a lot of intermarriage between the two families, especially later on. The Ottoman princes and princesses were all Imperial Highnesses, but Egyptian princes and princesses were only Highnesses.

Later, King Fouad downgraded us to Nabils and Nabilas, except for his immediate family, brothers and sisters, son and daughters who were Royal Highnesses. Precedence was according to how near one was related to the King. He did allow one prince per branch of the rest of the family, but they were only Highnesses. It may sound puerile, but it was the cause of a lot of bad blood, and divided the family from the ruler, which was later to be ominous. Mummy told us that King Fouad considered himself the Head of the Family and not just the king, and that any problems should be brought to him and that he would always be available to Family members. This changed when he married Queen Nazli. Not being a member of the Family, she disliked most of them and pretended to have a headache whenever a visitor appeared. This also meant that many of the younger members never met Prince Farouk and his sisters until much later.

Dad made the relationship with King Fouad worse by championing the poor. In 1934, he wrote an open letter in the newspapers to the King warning him that if he were not careful blood would run in the streets. He believed that providing the poorer classes with a decent livelihood would avoid communism. He had organised a Labour movement with a titular head because a member of the Royal Family could not be involved in politics. The King took this as a personal insult, and when Daddy drove out the first tram following the successful conclusion of a tram strike and the "Battle of Garden City" where workers and the police had clashed, he stripped him of his title of nabil and sent him to jail. Mum was in Alexandria and rushed back to Cairo to try to have him released. King Fouad was Mum's great uncle, her grandmother's brother, but he was very strict and did not play games. In the meantime, Mummy visited Dad in prison, bringing him food, mail, new records, to the delight of the press, who had taken up permanent residence outside the prison. Then he went on a hunger strike and the King decided this

Prince Abbas Halim in a beret after his title was removed by King Fouad. He was awarded the title "Sharif" by the people

was worse than having him free, so my father was duly released and sent home in an aura of glory, but no title.

Dad did not want the Labour movement to turn into a political party. The Wafd, posing as the nationalist party, saw a marvellous occasion to cash in, defending the poor and annoying the King in one go. The struggle between Dad and the Wafd involved many complications and a great deal of changing of sides by self-serving leaders of various syndicates.

On King Fouad's death, Prince Youssef Kamal, one of the older and most respected members of the Family, told Dad that his title would be restored if he left the Labour movement. He refused, but King Farouk restored it anyway.

Dad certainly took Mummy down an adventurous and often dangerous road. She soon got used to his occasional jail sentences, and took it all with a certain gallant panache. She thoroughly enjoyed herself most of the time. Daddy was far from being a faithful husband, but she was skilful in ridding herself of rivals. When we were older, Totes told us about a rumour that before meeting Mum, Dad had been married to a very beautiful and rather flighty English woman. We never dared ask either of our parents whether this was true. Mummy would have denied her very existence. Mummy was the Wife, the only Wife and nothing but the Wife.

The Family had one great drawback: all the princes and nabils considered at one point or other that they or their fathers should have reigned. The present incumbent was considered useless but to help him was not even envisaged. They had much more fun insulting him in private and telling ghastly stories about him without realising that they were digging their own grave, cutting off the branch on which they were sitting. To be a prince, you must have a reigning king. There were many intelligent, well-educated men among the princes, but they were proud and to offer assistance to the king who might refuse it would have been too much. A notable exception was Prince Omar

Toussoun but he died in 1944 before the situation became dramatic.

Dad's father, Prince Ibrahim, did not have much in the way of a fortune. He and Granny, Princess Ulfette Osman Fazil, remained married until the death of their daughter, Bedia, who adored her father. The marriage had not been a success. All Granny would say was how ugly he was. He was not that ugly, but he wore horrible glasses which did nothing to enhance his looks. When their daughter died, they divorced with no fuss. We did not see much of our grandfather. I believe it was more Dad's fault, but we never found out why. Prince Ibrahim married a German lady with whom he had a daughter Nimet and a son called Zeki. Zeki we did see because he adored Dad and would visit us often. Later they were estranged, again we had no idea why.

Dad's uncle, Saïd Halim Pasha, Grand Vizir of the Ottoman Empire under Sultan Mohamed V, had been arrested in 1919 by the British and deported to Malta with his brother Prince Mohamed Abbas Halim. All their assets in Egypt were confiscated. Saïd Halim was assassinated in 1921 in Rome by an Armenian terrorist.

After the war, the British would not let Dad back into Egypt because he had fought on the Turco-German side. When he finally returned, Prince Ismail Daoud took him Big Game hunting in Setit Valley in 1923 and in Mesopotamia and Somalia in 1925. He met the Duke and Duchess of York in a camp next to his. The future King George VI did not much like hunting but the Duchess as a true Scott was a good shot. Dad brought home various stag heads, a lion and a black buffalo. The lion is not the most dangerous animal to hunt, but the black buffalo, whose head still graces our dining room wall. It is fearless and will charge you at an incredible speed, so that you'd better not be in its line of vision! Prince Daoud found himself in this position and escaped by climbing a tree, while Dad roared with laughter.

Dad was an aeroplane pilot, racing driver, yachtsman and an all round

In Italy

sportsman in polo, golf, tennis and squash. Although he did not give up politics, he was much more discreet, avoiding clashes with the police and dramatic gestures. His Labour Party still existed, but with various uncontroversial official heads. He did not lose interest in it, but was now involved in sports. He believed in the theory that sports could be another way to combat poverty.

He sponsored or was patron of many sports: swimming and diving, riding, boxing, fencing, golf, car racing, cycling, football, flying and gliding. On November 9, 1935, he welcomed Antoine de Saint-Exupéry, one of the first flyers, at Almaza airport. In May 1941, he became President of the Royal Automobile Club of Egypt. In March 1947, he organised a Grand Prix Race in Cairo around Guezira. There were 16 cars with world famous drivers, such as Chiron, Nuvolari, Taruffi, Dusio. He even persuaded the King to attend and give the prizes.

As President of the Royal Automobile Club and the Touring Club, he was heavily involved in traffic regulations and the police. He lobbied in vain for better pay for the police. A well-paid police force can be counted on to ensure our safety. With such miserable salaries and large families that often go hungry who can blame them for taking tips for such innocent trespasses as being badly parked. He started a fund where drivers donated money to the Cairo and Alexandria police to provide them with life insurance.

Dad was also President of the Bridge Federation. Tournaments took place at the Royal Automobile Club, which was also a social club. Dad, although far from a snob, was very choosy as far as members were concerned. And he was very strict about Club rules. When Ulvia and I had guests who were not members, we were restricted to a special bar and restaurant. Even our famous movie stars, Anwar Wagdi and Leila Mourad could not break this rule.

I found thank-you letters for sponsoring or donating a cup from Collège

Prince Abas Halim with the boxing team, Sambo is kneeling

Saint-Marc of Alexandria, the Union Internationale des Sociétés sportives in Alex, the Associazone Sportiva Italiana, Rome and Alexandria, for a bicycle race between Alexandria and Kafr el Dawar, and the Racing Club de France.

Our chauffeur, Sambo, had been a boxer and Dad's assistant, Loutfia el Nadi, was our first woman flyer. Swimming was another area where Egyptians distinguished themselves as well as in squash, weightlifting and Greco-Roman wrestling. Dad tried to pull the poor out of their misery with the possibility of distinguishing themselves in something positive that would ensure better living conditions and better health. It engendered enthusiasm and a will to win.

And many did win. Ishak Hilmy swam the English Channel. At the Olympic Games in Amsterdam, Sayed Nosseir was first in middle-weight weightlifting, Moustapha Ibrahim first in Greco-Roman wrestling and in middle-weight. In springboard diving, Farid Simeika was third and in high diving he was named first, but it was so close that not until later was it announced that the American contestant had won. Our fencers, Cicurel and Mayal were among the ten best in the world. The Egyptian flag was raised twice on the central mast while the National Anthem was played. Then a third time for Simeika's third place. Everybody was so proud. Then Abdulla Neguib and Mohamed Sultan won first place as a team and Abdulla Neguib won first place individually in pigeon-shooting at the Match des Nations in Deauville, a prestigious venue. Egyptian athletes were greatly admired for their impeccable manners and excellent discipline. Then Mr. Agathou won the World Championship for target shooting. Edmond Soussa, the painter, was a champion billiards player and won for Egypt many times. Abdel Kerim in squash was world champion for years. We also had a tennis champion in Adly Shafei.

I found a photograph taken at the Egyptian Lawn Tennis Championships in 1951 with Field Marshal Viscount Montgomery, the British Ambassador Sir Ralph Stevenson and Lady Stevenson, surrounded by a group of British officers

Princess Tawhida after a visit to Prince Abbas Halim in prison

Princess Fatma, daughter of Khedive Ismail

seated in one of the central rows in the Centre Court at the Guezira Sporting Club. Daddy is not far from him to the right, and my cousin Aleya and I a trifle lower down. Other friends and acquaintances can be seen nearby. None of us seem to realise that the Great Man was amongst us!

Dad was President of the Civil Aviation Association, the Egyptian Olympic Athletic Club, the Poids et Haltères Club, the Union egyptienne des Sociétés sportives, and President of the Egyptian Lawn Tennis Association. Mummy was Vice President and President of the Umpires Association.

Everything interested him. He had expertise in the most surprising areas. We have piles of plans and suggestions for better and safer roads, traffic regulations, ideas to combat poverty and corruption, and enhance the lives of the poor.

**

But he was not the only member of the Family trying to help the country. Most notably there was Prince Omar Toussoun. He made huge strides in land reclamation in the Governorate of Beheira where he built model villages on every piece of reclaimed land. These were connected not only to a small railway line, but also by roads which were lined with trees to protect the peasants from the sun as they walked home.

He was active in politics, especially when the British took over everything in Egypt, the police, administration, ministries and finances. Instead of leaving, they were here to stay. Prince Omar wrote a book castigating the British for the bombing of Alexandria in 1882, but also criticising the Egyptian leaders for misleading information on the condition of the forts. This resulted in the destruction of much of Alexandria and the death of 700 Egyptians as opposed to six Englishmen.

Prince Omar Toussoun

Prince Youssef Kemal

Princes of the Royal Family: from left (front) Mohamed Ali Halim, Mohamed Ali Tewfik, Abdel Moneim, Ibrahim Halim; (middle) Ismail Daoud, Amr Ibrahim, Said Toussoun, Mohamed Ali Ibrahim, Abbas Halim, Prince Ismail Hussein, Said Daoud; (back) Alaeddin Muchtar, Mansour Daoud, Soliman Daoud, Mahmoud el Sioufi Bey, the third Chamberlain.

Prince Omar Toussoun was in agreement with Moustapha Kamel and his National Party demanding independence from the British and the unity of the Nile valley. At the end of World War I, on hearing President Wilson's declaration that all nations had a right to self-determination, Prince Omar wanted to send a delegation to Versailles to plead Egypt's case. He was advised to discuss the idea with Saad Zaghloul Pasha of the Wafd, but Zaghloul was not ready to share an eventual success with a member of the Royal Family. King Fouad, afraid that Prince Omar had an eye on the throne, ordered Prince Omar not to participate. Prince Omar had actively supported Moustapha Kamel and then Mohamed Farid of the old National Party and wanted all the different parties to unite in the interests of Egypt. This was not to be and it never is.

Prince Omar wanted to secure the country's borders, especially with the Sudan. He considered the unity of the Nile valley as primordial for Egypt as the source of its water. He was horrified by the Italian conquest of Libya and Abyssinia and worried by the disintegration of the Ottoman Empire and the emerging situation in Palestine. What a loss to Egypt that he could not prevail.

Prince Youssef Kemal was another wealthy man who felt it was his duty to look after his people and his country and to contribute to their welfare. After the revolution, he brought back the money he had placed in Europe and was rewarded by losing all his possessions. Prince Mohamed Ali Tewfik, the Crown Prince before the birth of Prince Ahmed Fouad, collected a vast assortment of Islamic treasures in his house at Manial in Cairo and cultivated rare trees and plants in his garden. The whole was donated to the country. Earlier, Princess Fatma, one of Khedive Ismail's daughters, sold her fabulous collection of jewels to build Cairo University. The Queen and the Princesses headed the Mohamed Ali Foundation and were very active in charity work. When the revolution came, everybody conveniently forgot all this.

Im Auftrage des Führers und Reichskanzlers

beehre ich mich,

S. Hoheit d. Prinzen Abbas Halim

zu dem vom 5.—12. September 1938 stattfindenden

Reichsparteitag

nach Nürnberg einzuladen.

Der Stellvertreter des Führers

Rudolf Heß

Die Antwort wird auf beiliegender Vordruckkarte erbeten bis zum 25. August 1938 an das Amt
für Ehrengäste - Stellv. Gauleiter Gerland - Nürnberg, Grandhotel.

Invitation from the Führer

The public did not know much about this. They considered the rich princes must have stolen everything they possessed. They cannot be blamed because that was the norm for many of the pashas and beys. Some were former fellahin who had doublecrossed their masters and at times even ruined them. Once rich, they did not care what happened to their erstwhile equals.

* * *

In September 1938, our last summer in England before the War, Daddy was invited to Nuremberg by Hitler. I have no idea through what channels this invitation was sent, but I suppose as a former officer in the German Army in WWI, he must have been listed somewhere. Mum says he was "asked by Goering to make an inspection of the factories in Germany to note what Germany had in the way of airplanes. Abbas brought back a report which he later discussed with the people at the English Speaking Union in London, where we had lunch one day. He told them, what Lindbergh had previously said, that this was a very dangerous business. But people laughed at him and called him a defeatist. He repeatedly said: 'I'm telling you what I've seen with my own eyes.'" In Cairo, he told the British about his factory visits in Germany. They would not believe him either.

What is either overlooked or avoided these days is the fact that a great many distinguished visitors travelled to Germany at that time. In Sir Henry Channon's diary for August-September 1936, we find him and his wife, Lady Honor Guinness, being entertained by Goering and his wife at a banquet at the Berlin Opera House. Present were the Crown Prince of Italy, the Crown Prince of Sweden and the King of Bulgaria. Prince Philip of Hesse introduced the Channons to Goering at the latter's request. Next day, the Channons lunched with Rippentrop at his house. There was another Goering party at

The Lord Chamberlain is
commanded by Their Majesties to invite

Sa Seigneurie La Nabil Ibrahin Italian &
La Nabila Italian

to an Afternoon Party in the Garden of

Buckingham Palace on Thursday, the 25th July, 1929,

from 4 to 6.30 p.m. (Weather Permitting)

Morning Dress.

Invitation from King George V

the Ministerium this time. Not to be outdone, next evening was the Goebbels party for 2000 guests, with magnificent fireworks after dinner. The German Imperial Family was also represented by the Crown Princess and "Fritzi", Prince Friedrich of Prussia, the Kaiser's grandson. Queen Victoria's grandson, the Duke of Saxe-Coburg-Gotha, a fervent Nazi, had given up his title of Duke of Albany when he decided to remain German.

All this is to show just how many were taken in by Hitler. They could not reconcile the person they met socially with the homicidal maniac who soon ruled most of Europe. In Albert Speer's book *Inside the Third Reich*, he describes his initial admiration of Hitler and how long it took him to see the truth. Of course, he did not want to see the truth. I suppose for people not living in Germany it was even easier to avoid the truth.

***

But Daddy was really interested in Egypt and the poor. He had the right ideas, but they were difficult to implement in the existing political conditions. We were under British rule, and make no mistake about it. And it's nearly always a mistake to go against your own class or group, a "Philippe Egalité" never wins. Whether you like it or not, you are hemmed in by your position. The War stopped any possibility of real democracy in Egypt thanks to the British and their precarious situation when Rommel was outside Alexandria. Sir Miles Lampson did not even pretend that the country was independent. He rode roughshod over the King and everybody else. To this day, it's difficult to forgive Lampson. He killed a whole generation's dreams and hopes. He took away our self-respect. And he ruined our King.

So I suppose Dad decided to return to his World War I side, which after all was the favourite of most Egyptians. All I can say is that my parents' attitude

*Prince Abbas Halim, Sir Miles Lampson and Count Mazzolini,
the Italian Ambassador*

was ambiguous. Of course, they owed their loyalty only to Egypt. Once the Nazi horrors had been filmed and photographed, there was no way to deny them. There is no excuse, no reason, no intellectual twisting and turning, no argument that can explain how so many people managed to turn into monsters. Compared to the other shameful acts that so-called human beings have perpetrated, like the Spanish Inquisition, the French Revolution, the various massacres that have occurred and are still taking place to this day, the Holocaust stands out as the worst as well as the most efficient extermination enacted by man on man while ensuring the greatest possible mental and physical agony. I'm sure that most of us cannot understand how bloodthirsty we really are. The fate of the Jews reached limits never surpassed, but the pleasure that crowds take watching hangings, beheadings, fights of all sorts, preferably with a little torture involved, says nothing much for our humanity.

With General Rommel nearing Alexandria and the Allies doing badly everywhere else, Sir Miles had orders to get tough with the anti-British contingent. Daddy, Prince Farouk of the Imperial Ottoman Family, Taher Pasha, a cousin of our parents, and Ali Maher Pasha, an occasional Prime Minister, were consigned to house arrest. Not in their own houses, but one chosen by the government. Daddy and Prince Farouk, comrades in arms since the First World War, were together in a house in Ayat, an hour's drive from Cairo, belonging to the Boutros Ghali family. Much later, Ulvia's daughter married into that family.

Dad had an unusual amount of patience that carried him through some bad moments, especially after the revolution. And he would never complain. When something was impossible to avoid, he believed spending one's energy fighting it was stupid.

He was extremely well-read in five languages. A measure of his understanding of national and international events were the people he met.

Princes Mansour Daoud, Abbas Halim and Abdel Moneim with Cherif Sabry Pasha

Prince Abbas Halim, Lady Lampson, Prince Ismail Daoud and
Prince Amr Ibrahim at the Guezira Sporting Club

We have photos of him with Vishinsky at a cocktail party, at Moussadek's bedside, with Couve de Murville, the French Ambassador and future Minister of Foreign Affairs and Prime Minister of France, and everybody in Egypt of course, important and not important. We even found a letter from Russell Pasha, former British Head of Cairo Police, asking him to help a policeman, who is being thrown out of his job at the retirement age of 60 with 6 months pay and no pension. Russell Pasha asks Dad to help him find work for this "faithful old government servant."

Dad did not have a snobbish bone in his body. It's tragic he never had the possibility and power to go on with the good work. After the revolution, nothing more could be done.

***

Our "private family", as we called ourselves, thought of the house in Garden City as our real home. It was a large house, but not a palace. The rooms had very high ceilings and were generally huge, as were the bathrooms. The house was built at the narrow point of a triangle covering one feddan, with the rest forming the garden. Trees along the boundaries gave some privacy. The garden itself was mostly lawn, with herbaceous borders along the edges and smaller trees and flowering bushes scattered throughout.

The house really belonged to Mummy, given to her by Grandpa. Despite its size, it was a home. She ran it with well-ordered severity, which gave us a sense of security.

There were beautiful things, such as the three Gobelin tapestries in the hall, less beautiful things and downright shabby things. Our rooms, the schoolroom and upstairs hall were in the last category. Considering how we treated the furniture, Mummy thought it useless to renew anything. Apart from engraving

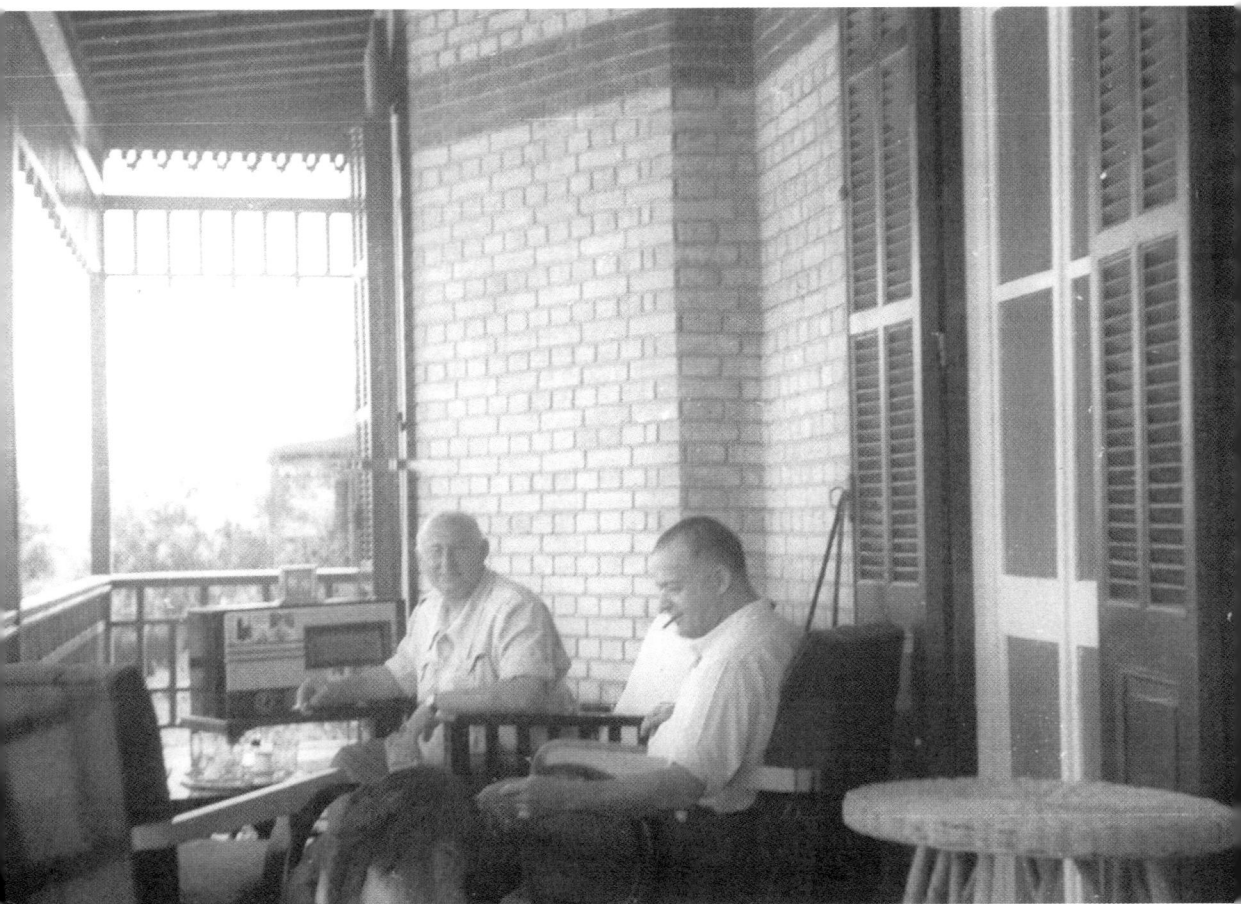

Prince Abbas Halim with Farouk Effendi, son of Sultan Abdel Meguid II,
interned in Ayat

our names on the tables, generally embellished with such lamentable descriptives as "pig", "idiot" and "sneak", we tore the paper off the walls of Ulvia's room and the carpets bore testimony to everything from Castor Oil and Scott's Emulsion to ink and plasticine. As we outgrew the more dangerous manifestations of hooliganism, Mummy cautiously redid our rooms one by one, according to our age.

I was first, being the eldest. Mum made a lovely room for me, all pink satin and white tulle, with a small desk and a sofa with two easy chairs. The room had been Grandpa's and had a separate entrance from the hall and a private bathroom. The bathroom was enormous: besides the usual amenities, there was plenty of space for a huge white cupboard. Both it and my bedroom had balconies, which could never be used due to the screams emanating from boys at the Ibrahimia school which had been built next door. Unfortunately, these boys could also see us when we were in the garden and our every appearance produced horrendous yelling and cat-calls. Later on, we met some of the boys and roundly insulted them.

Ulvia's room was blue satin with white tulle. Mummy knew her tomboy daughter and did not go to too much trouble. The room was soon a shambles. For Ali she did not even try.

The kitchen and rooms for the male servants were in the cellar, not completely underground, its windows gave onto an open space under the first floor, but it was dark. In the attic was the ironer's room and bedrooms for the female servants. The back stairs were wood and rickety. There were half-floor rooms where the dressmaker or some other visitor could work.

Downstairs everything was quiet and orderly. In summer, the sun shone through the drawn-down but pushed-out shutters, *jalousies* we called them then, settling in long stripes on the carpet, giving a muted Mediterranean feel to the rooms and a cool underwater light to the house, exquisite relief from

Garden City house and garden

Princess Tawhida Halim in the sitting room

Prince Abbas Halim in the study

Garden City house lit up for King Farouk's wedding, January 1938

the blazing heat outside. There was a Venetian glass window above the staircase which shed slivers of brilliant red, green and gold over the hall. The only sound was the occasional buzzing of a tired fly.

At one o'clock sharp, lunch was served in the dark mahogany dining room hung with green velvet curtains embroidered in gold. We sat at a long refectory table, my mother presiding in a huge, straight-backed "throne." Silver candelabra with silver shepherds and dogs gambolling around the base, silver birds to hold the salt and pepper stood on the polished surface, and individual embroidered organdy or lace mats were placed under each plate and glass. The china was blue and gold Limoges. And the cook was an all-round *cordon bleu*, excelling both in French and local cuisine.

The living room where my parents entertained a "chosen few" had a covered veranda giving on the garden. It was smallish, with comfortable brown velvet cushions on brown leather armchairs and sofa. The coffee table was an elephant's ear and the waste paper basket an elephant's foot. The tusks held an old Turkish mirror. My father's other hunting trophies hung on the walls. A huge black buffalo was especially impressive, but the most frightening, and the cause of countless childhood nightmares, was the stuffed lion. He lay in majestic dignity to the left of the door as you walked in. One of our favourite amusements was to lure our friends into the room, preferably with the lights lowered, yell warnings and once we were sure they had noticed the lion, we vanished.

Opposite was the music room, which my mother later bestowed on me as my private sanctum. If one of the "kids", i.e. Ulvia or Ali, was unwise enough to enter without invitation, they would be beaten up without mercy. Once I nearly killed Ulvia by banging her head against a marble-topped table. Mummy was in the vicinity and hearing the screams came rushing and fortunately saved her, but as she had no idea who the guilty one was, Ulvia was slapped and I got off as usual. When I was not trying to kill my siblings,

I practised on the Bechstein baby grand piano. The length of time I spent practising was in direct proportion to the direction my latest ambition had taken. I had a collection of beautiful art books and it gave me the idea of becoming a painter. I was hopeless, and despite my extraordinary powers of self-deception, I finally realised the sad truth.

Next to the music room, communicating through a door behind the piano, was the library, a very large room with three French windows giving on the front gate. The walls were covered with cream-coloured wooden shelves, overflowing with all types of books. My mother, dressed in green velvet, a long pearl necklace held negligently in her left hand, painted by Edmond Soussa, surveyed you from the wall over the fireplace. There were comfortable chairs and sofas and a large desk which nobody ever used. I sneaked in as often as possible and read everything I could get my hands on, probably hoping to come across a dirty book of sorts, but apart from a rather scandalous one on Empress Elizabeth of Austria, I found nothing. Grandpa's collection on French theatre was my favourite. I became intimate with Sarah Bernhardt, La Duse, Madame Réjane. My other heroes were Rosemeyer the auto-racer and Amelia Earhart, the pilot. She remained my idol for a relatively long time—one could always dream of flying!

*　*　*

Until the War, winters were spent in Cairo and summers in England, living in Nanny's house outside Poole in Dorset. Nanny was Miss Alice Marsh and she had built a bungalow next to the house of her sister and her husband, Beryl and Frank. We loved going there and loved going to church on Sunday. My mother had no idea we were going to church regularly and had a fit when she found out. Poor Nanny got the scolding of her life. We were Moslems and

Nevine, Ulvia and Mohamed Ali in Garden City

not supposed to go to church. I was stunned as I had fallen in love with the vicar, but not for long. One Sunday, Nanny invited him to tea in the garden and he fell off his chair. A vicar, or any man of God, should not be undignified enough to fall off his chair, no matter how derelict the chair.

The mix-up concerning our religion was certainly the fault of my parents as we received no religious education at all. Granny, my paternal grandmother, finally took matters into her own hands and made us learn the main Moslem prayers by heart phonetically, as we could not read Arabic. Our parents did not want us to learn Arabic too early as it would ruin our pronunciation in other languages, a piece of idiocy that has haunted us ever since.

I was over three years older than Ulvia and five years older than Ali. Mummy decided I needed a governess rather than a nurse. She hired Miss Eileen MacConachie. She was very lame, but so pretty with her beautiful skin and blonde hair. She was also a fine tactician with us children. She could do nothing with Nanny, of course, who resented her terribly and never forgave her for taking her "Pussy" away from her. Nanny had her own names for us: I was Pussy, Ulvia was Patsy and Ali was Peter. Some of our very oldest friends still remember.

I loved Nanny terribly since I was a very young child, she was my refuge and ally. When I had nightmares she let me creep into her bed in the middle of the night. My parents were not around much in the nursery. My mother was a good mother, but in those days people who could afford it hired nannies and governesses to look after their children, especially being members of the Royal Family we were to be educated at home. Totes, born 28 September 1920, being so much older and not technically a "Royal", first went to boarding school in England and then to Victoria College in Alexandria, a British public school inaugurated in 1909 by Queen Victoria's son, the Duke of Connaught.

With the arrival of Miss MacConachie, immediately baptised Con, I was

Nevine with Nanny

upgraded to Nevine. Another improvement thanks to Con was in our Channel crossing. Nanny always herded us into the cabin below deck, where we lay on bunks, watching and hearing everybody being frightfully sick and promptly following suit. Thanks to Con, we were liberated from this torture and taken up on deck in the fresh air. Much to Nanny's disappointment, we were never ill again,

In Poole, we stayed with Beryl and Frank because Nanny's house was not ready. Frank was a farmer with kind, rough manners, Beryl was a tall, angular woman, kinder than she looked. She brought us a cup of tea and a slice of bread and butter early in the morning before breakfast. They had a piano and an organ in the front parlour and Frank would sometimes play the organ for us.

To this day I remember the smell of chicken feed. It consisted of potato peel with bread crumbs and vegetable leftovers. I loved the smell. The kitchen was small and opened straight into the garden, with the outhouse nearby. It was only when we moved into Nanny's house that we had a real bathroom. The new house was in the same garden as Frank's, scarcely a garden but rather a wilderness. There were a few fruit trees and vegetable patches and it was fenced in by wire haphazardly strung up any which way. The moors began immediately at the back of the house, streaked with red cart lanes.

When Con arrived, we bought an old caravan for her to live in as there was not enough room in Nanny's house and anyway, Nanny hated Con. Of course, we children would have loved to live in the caravan. It had a front and back door, little curtained windows, two berths and a wash basin.

The front of Nanny's house gave onto a small lane. A neighbour took me for a ride in the side-car of his motorcycle one day, just after Lawrence of Arabia had killed himself on one. Nanny considered them infernal machines and was frantic with worry until I got back. She was not far wrong as there were a great many ghastly accidents involving motorcycles and to this day.

Our parents managed to spend a few days with us in the summer, and when I was seven, they drove me back to London with them. I was ecstatic when Mummy and her friend, Lady Brougham took me to a pantomime. Mum said I sat watching the stage absolutely motionless during the entire performance.

She took me shopping during that trip. London was renowned for its marvellous children's clothes and I was soon the proud owner of new shoes, hats, dresses and coats. I had a beautiful pink silk dress, pleated from the shoulders down, with a pink ribbon on each shoulder; another was in organdy embroidered with small bunches of flowers. There was a light beige coat with a brown velvet collar and cuffs and one in blue velvet with a hat to match. Then lots of shoes: white, blue and black with straps. I was beside myself with joy and the day I had to return to Poole, there was a dreadful scene. My parents were invited to join friends in Scotland and could not put off their departure. And they had spoilt me enormously. Con was to take me back and she finally persuaded me to spend a few days at her mother's house in Worthing. I got into the train with great reluctance and after all the crying promptly fell asleep. A huge tea with crumpets, muffins and scones did a lot to reconcile me with life. Con took me to an amusement park in New Haven, where you could drive yourself in little boats. The Sussex countryside was really beautiful, very different from Dorset. Con took me to visit a friend of hers who was governess in a real castle surrounded by rolling green downs amid century old trees.

The summer after, my parents took me to Oatlands Park in Kent. It had been a royal residence and was now a luxury hotel. We were joined there by the Finneys, Harold and Helen, old friends of my parents. Harold's father Oswald was deeply involved in both real estate and cotton in Egypt. Their two daughters, Joan and Ann, accompanied them and I was extremely annoyed that being a few years older than me they could dine downstairs with the grown-ups. One night there was a Gala dinner and I made a huge fuss about

The caravan

not being able to go with them. To pacify me, Mummy left the number of the Reception to call if I needed anything. I racked my brains to find a good excuse and at last came up with a spider on the ceiling. I called Reception and in no time, they all trooped into my room, curious as to the reason for my call. The spider story went down badly and to my fury, they all laughed heartily and left. That was our last year in England before the War.

***

Back in Cairo, Mummy fired Nanny. Poor Nanny was the victim of the intrigues going on between nurses, governess and servants. When she came to say goodbye to me, her darling, her Pussy, I turned my face to the wall and would not kiss her. She was nearly in tears, as I am as I write this. I had been told that she had said nasty things about Mummy and I could not forgive that. She sent me Christmas cards for years, but I never answered. Con, who had so successfully turned me against Nanny, was to suffer the same fate a little later. This time it was because Mummy had decided Con belonged to MI6 or whatever the British Secret Service was called at that time.

The summer of 1939, Mummy was very ill with an abscess in her lung, caused by her teeth. We all went to Switzerland where she was being treated in a clinic in Berne. We three children with Con and Miss Faganelli, a Yugoslav governess for Ulvia and Ali, were shipped off to Zurich, then to Thun and Interlaken. Granny, her sister Auntie Tabby (Tante Bedia) and their niece, Auntie Mi (Emine) supervised us.

I remember Switzerland well, after all I was nine. I loved the lakes and our boat trips, the Jungfrau, Mönch and Eiger which we could see so well from our hotel windows in Interlaken. There was Spietz, a tiny village on Lake Thun, where the boat always stopped. My favourite was Zurich. We lived at

91

the Waldhaus Dolder Hotel and Con took me to the International Fair which had just opened, another marvel, with so many exciting things to do: small boats and cars to ride and little trains to visit the various sites. There were also aerial cabins crossing the lake, but I was not allowed on them, too dangerous.

Then Granny found Ali locked up in a cupboard, a dire day for Miss Faganelli. We learned that whenever they were naughty she had the nasty habit of locking Ulvia and more often poor little Ali in a cupboard. She was promptly fired, and Con and Auntie Mi looked after us until we got a temporary replacement, a very pretty young thing called Miss Fränelli. We would have liked to have had her permanently. Luckily for her, this did not happen. We were at the top of the list of Monstrous Children compiled by the Cairo Governesses Association.

On September 1st, 1939, Germany invaded Poland and on September 3rd, England declared war on Germany. Thank heavens Mummy was much better and we were all in Berne and packed up. We took a train to Genoa and the last boat of the Khedivial Mail Line home. Grandpa Yeghen was President of the Khedivial Mail Line, so no problem. But Auntie Tabby, who had severe asthma, lived in Switzerland because she could not stand the heat and dust of Egypt. With Auntie Mi, her brother's daughter who had lived with her ever since the divorce of her parents, they spent the entire war in Switzerland.

***

A happy event before the War was the engagement and wedding of King Farouk to Safinaz Zulfikar in 1938. The excitement and joy of all classes in Egypt was unbelievable. It began on his accession in 1936. He was young, handsome, and keen to be a good ruler. Everybody loved him because he gave them hope. When his engagement to Safinaz was announced, joy knew no

Princess Bedia, daughter of Prince Osman, son of Prince Mustapha Fazil,
son of Ibrahim I

bounds. The photograph of the engaged couple was in every house, shop, car, café, and office. In the official photograph, the future queen wore a dress with a high collar and the King was in white tie and a *tarboush*, or fez.

When I learned I was to attend the wedding, I walked around in a blissful haze. Then a terrible disappointment: I was not to be a bridesmaid and my mother made me wear a short dress, when all the other girls of my age were wearing long dresses. This was brought home at the Palace, when Princess Fathia, the King's youngest sister and my age but wearing a long dress, refused to have anything to do with me.

I did attend a "real" Egyptian wedding with my best friend Nanou, Nawal Zaki, later Princess Saïd Toussoun. Nanou's parents had rented one of the Finney houses in Alexandria, dark pink and built in a row, at right angles to the Corniche, near the house where the wedding was taking place. We rushed off before anybody could prevent us and were ushered in to see the bride. She looked terrified, dressed all in white, her face smothered in white powder. She was soon to undergo the "virgin" test, by which the husband would make sure that she was pure. Without going into sordid details, if the material he used bore blood stains, honour was saved. It was all rather impressive because drums began to roll while the "test" was being prepared and took quite a long time. Finally, they reached a crescendo, the yulluleing began and all was well.

Nothing like this happened at the reception at Koubbeh Gardens Palace. Beginning in the early evening. Queen Nazli, the Queen Mother, received the ladies in the big entrance hall of the Palace. Mummy had given me precise instructions concerning protocol. Queen Nazli would receive us and I was to kiss her hand and that was all.

On the great day, Mummy and I were driven to Koubbeh Palace by our chauffeur Sambo. I remember the big hall with the King and the new Queen standing in the rear, surrounded by their bridesmaids. Queen Nazli came

The Royal Wedding

Queen Farida

Queen Nazli

Camel troops during the military parade in Abdine Square celebrating the wedding

Royal reception: (from left) Prince Abbas Halim, unknown, Princess Nimet Muchtar, Princess Faiza, Queen Nazli, Princess Fawzia, Queen Farida, King Farouk, Sultana Melek

forward to greet us, wearing a red sequin evening gown, which shone as brightly as her jewels. After dutifully kissing her hand, I found her so beautiful that I threw my arms around her neck and kissed her cheek. Mummy was horrified and excused herself to the Queen. Luckily I was a pretty little girl and Queen Nazli was very kind and kissed me back. My cousin Hassan Hassan wrote in his book *In the House of Muhammad Ali* that he did exactly the same thing. The beautiful Queen was certainly a great success with children.

After the guests had arrived, the newly-weds descended the Palace steps leading to the garden, stopping at the bottom for the King and officers of the armed forces to salute the flag while the National Anthem was played.

The King and Queen then walked through the grounds to a tent where dinner was served. No alcohol of course, but otherwise it was like any European royal reception, except for the magnificent outfits worn by the waiters, long red robes embroidered with gold thread and red *tarboushes* to top it all off. I can't remember walking to the tent. I was probably sent home.

I cut out all the photographs I could lay my hands on of the wedding, the new Queen, and the festivities from papers and magazines, but I lost them during one of our moves, to my eternal regret. I pestered my mother to buy me material similar to the Queen's wedding dress, which was in silver brocade. Mummy thought this heroine worship a little overdone and when Princess Fawzia married the Shahpur in 1939, she was resigned to going through another frenzy. Funnily, I was much less excited by this wedding. Not only was I not invited, but I found the bridegroom's nose much too big, and certainly King Farouk was much more handsome.

Small light bulbs were festooned around our house when the King married, a considerable concession on the part of my parents who were usually on bad terms with the sovereign. With the new King, they had not yet had time to oppose him.

The town was a fairyland, what with official decorations and private efforts. A few days after the wedding, the King and Queen appeared on the balcony of Abdine Palace to wave to the crowd gathered below. The enthusiasm was tremendous and the affection was almost palpable. For the first time, the Queen wore the *yashmak*, the organdy veil which covers the chin and mouth. In her engagement pictures and at her wedding, she wore no veil, except just before the ceremony as is customary at any wedding. Once married, the veil is thrown back. The *yashmak* is supposed to be worn by the Queen, Princesses, wives of ministers, etc. on all official occasions, such as opening of hospitals, schools, visits to members of the Royal Family. This did not include the Girl Scouts, of which the Queen was the Head and here she wore a beret. The ladies always complained about the *yashmak*, but you could wear it as low or as high as you liked and for an unattractive woman, it was a godsend. As a means of concealing the features of the Queen, Princesses, etc. it was, of course, a total failure and only a sop to possible criticism by the religious element.

The King took his wife everywhere, often driving himself on unofficial occasions, and to all the balls and receptions given after the wedding. His two older sisters, Fawzia and Faiza were also allowed to attend some functions. His mother was completely independent, leading to later disaster.

We children saw the Queens at Granny's. She never went out and as one of the older princesses she rated a visit from the Queens. Queen Nazli liked Granny very much and Granny liked her, to everybody's surprise as they could not have been more dissimilar.

The great excitement was the visit of the new Queen. She arrived in a red Palace car, preceded by motorcycle police and accompanied by a lady-in-waiting. We'd opened both sides of the garden gate so that the car could stop at the stairs leading to the front door. Granny was waiting at the top of the stairs to greet the Queen.

The Queen emerged from the car, wearing a white fox stole, a pale blue tulle evening dress and the *yashmak*. She looked gorgeous and we were stunned with admiration. Granny took her into the living room and it was only some time later that we were summoned to meet her. We kissed her hand and she kissed our cheeks. Ali in a Lord Fauntleroy suit, white velvet with a wide, white lace collar, looked adorable and she asked him for *Salam el Malek*, which means salute to the King. He had no idea what she meant, but he bowed very deeply. She laughed delightedly and told Granny what a darling little boy he was.

There was another big event after the wedding, the first Opening of Parliament of the new reign, where the ladies had to wear trains. Mummy had a gold lame dress and a blue velvet train with gold embroidery. Of course, she wore diamonds galore. Photos of the Queen show her wearing the famous diamond necklace and earrings plus decorations, in a lame sleeveless dress, a train embroidered with a peacock tail, edged with ermine, long white gloves and holding a large feathered fan. There were a great many occasions at that time when the dresses and jewels worn were breathtaking.

The Empress of Iran, our Princess Fawzia, was an exquisitely beautiful woman as you can see from her photographs. You can also see the fabulous jewels she is wearing, many presents from the Shah. The Iranian Imperial Family had the most amazing collection of precious stones in the world, with the Indian princes their only rivals. For the Shah's coronation in 1967, Van Cleef & Arpels of Paris won the competition to fashion the crown to be worn by Empress Farah, consisting of 1600 precious stones. Another famous jeweller much appreciated by both the Iranian and Egyptian Royal Families was Harry Winston. With him, one could be sure of receiving the most spectacular stones in the most fabulous settings.

Opening of Parliament

Cherif Sabry Pasha, Prince Abbas Halim, Ahmed Hassanein Pasha (standing), King Farouk, the Shahpur

Fawzia, Empress of Iran

Prince Abbas Halim with Prince Mohamed Ali Tewfik

The grim side soon appeared. The War reached Egypt. We were being bombed by the Germans and Italians. When the bombing started, Mum decided our house in Garden City was too near British Headquarters and rented it to the American Minister, Mr. Alexander Kirk. She then leased a house in Koubbeh Gardens, a Cairo suburb. This was a major error. Garden City was never bombed, while Koubbeh Gardens was quite regularly; and at the end of the War, it took her a long time to get her house back. Mr. Kirk did not want to move. As he had diplomatic immunity, she had to wait until he was good and ready. She even called Nahas Pasha, who refused to interfere, asking her if she wanted to create a diplomatic incident between Egypt and the United States. Mum pointed out that it was a house, not an oilfield.

I recently found my grandmother's 1942 diary from which I quote.

There was a crisis. The Prime Minister, Sirry Pasha, rushed between the Palace and *la présidence,* the Cabinet Office. Miles Lampson visited him several times. Then Sirry Pasha declared the sky had cleared. But Mummy visited Granny on February 5th and told her about the serious events of the day before. "At 9 p.m., Lampson and General Stone with British troops armed with machine guns surrounded the Palace and thanks to the British bayonets, the great patriot Nahas has been charged with forming a government, not as the King wished with a cabinet of all parties, but a purely Wafdist one. Parliament has been dissolved and new elections called. Lots of bla-bla from Nahas. He is saving Egypt from the horrors of war. The problems of supplies were caused by the previous Cabinet's lack of planning. Now the poor will be better fed than the rich. Under Wafdist governments, all the reserves of Egypt vanished, 40 million pounds worth."

Most of the Royal Family and a majority of Egyptians were pro-Axis because we were simply anti-British. We wanted our complete independence from Britain, had been put off umpteen times, or given vague promises, still they sat on the Suez Canal and during the war they were all over the place. The British Ambassador, Sir Miles Lampson, was particularly heavy-handed. King Farouk, young, handsome and very popular, was on bad terms with the pro-British Wafdist Nahas Pasha. The Wafd pretended to be the ultra-nationalist party of the people, demanding independence with demonstrations and assassinations which only put up the back of the British and placed the sovereign in an impossible position. The King was the first to want independence, but he, and his father before him, realised that assassinations were not the answer. Now the Wafd, in their usual self-serving way, sided with the British against the King. This was to be their undoing, and paved the way for the revolution.

Sir Miles stormed into the King's office, demanding he appoint Nahas as Prime Minister or abdicate. The King was about to sign, when Hassanein Pasha whispered to him. He stopped and agreed to nominate Nahas. This manner of treating "the boy" as Lampson called him, infuriated Egyptians who all closed ranks behind the King. Strangely, it was the military men like General Stone, who strongly objected to the use of force. They also objected to his rudeness in dealing with the King. But Sir Miles had Churchill and Eden on his side with carte blanche to continue his bullying.

Lady Diana Cooper, who with her husband Duff had been staying at the British Embassy during the famous evening of February 4th, commiserated with Sir Miles when he said "the boy" had agreed to his terms and therefore he had no excuse to oblige him to abdicate. To demonstrate how the British felt about us Egyptians, from our King on down, I quote from Lady Diana Cooper's book *Trumpets from the Steep* concerning February 4th: "Sir Miles has a first-rate political crisis boiling up on him. There have been students in the streets shouting 'Vive Rommel', 'A bas l'Angleterre' and 'Vive le Roi'. These presumably are the Fascist Palace pro-Italian party, I gather a very small one. The King wouldn't see the leader of the Wafd until the Palace was surrounded by tanks and machine guns, and a boat waiting to bear him, crownless, to Ceylon. Sir Miles went with some generals and a pistol for Pharaoh's head to insist on our advice being taken. In the other he carried an abdication drafted by the practised hand of Walter Monckton [he'd written the abdication paper for Edward VIII to sign]. Pen in hand the victim complained of the ink and then asked for another chance, so the tanks rolled home. When I came back from dining with my new favourite, Mr. Alexander Kirk, American Minister here, a dear freak [he wore violet suits] at 11 p.m. I found the Embassy hall a babble of huddled groups... H.E. came out of his den, dressed in pearl-gray frac, arm-in-arm with Nahas Pasha, both grinning themselves in two."

There was another run-in with Lampson at Cairo airport when the King went to receive his sister, the Empress of Iran, her daughter Shahnaz and her sister-in-law Ashraf with her daughter. Lampson and his wife as Allies, the Iranian Minister, and our Minister to Iran were also present. The King drove himself and took his mother, wife and sister back to Abdine, the others following. "As the reception was purely a family one, the Lampsons were *cut* it seems. More rage and ultimatum: apologies by Monday. Where are we going?" Nahas ironed out the incident, explaining that had the Lampsons spoken to him as Minister of Foreign Affairs, he would have told them it was a purely family affair. A month later, "another sister of the Shah has arrived, Princess Shams, daughter-in-law of the Iranian Ambassador. They have taken a liking to the country."

The King and other members of the Royal Family were distributing food to the poor. Princess Chevikiar, King Fouad's first wife, distributed food to

5000 people. We in Koubbeh were sewing dresses for girls and small galabeyas for boys, every Friday these clothes with food were given to the poor.

There were many parties, given by Princess Chevikiar, Aunt Emine Tugay, Aunt Ain-el-Hayat Ibrahim, another wealthy cousin of my parents. The King and Queen were always present, as were many very beautiful, high-born and not so high-born ladies. The King found himself in foreign territory: young, handsome and a king in the midst of enormous temptation. The Queen was extremely jealous and not sparing in her comments to her husband. Then she tried to make him jealous which Granny thought was a serious mistake.

There was another problem. Queen Nazli, free from a possessive, stern husband, was linked to various well-known men and her life style became scandalous. The King was quite unable to control his mother. The two queens came to hate each other. Queen Nazli had chosen Safinaz Zulfikar thinking she would be a submissive daughter-in-law. The two women quarrelled continuously and complained to the King. The poor man did not know where to turn, and when he did, it was the beginning of the downward path.

Meanwhile, the parties continued. Princess Samiha and her husband Wahid Yousry Pasha, the son of Princess Chevikiar and Seifullah Pasha Yousry, gave a fancy dress ball where Mum wore exactly the same dress as the doll she carried, all in pale blue taffeta, with a large hat. It seems this was a famous doll. Another at the Toussouns, where the ladies outshone themselves in their gorgeous dresses and superb jewels. Kadria Zaki, called Tata, Nawal Toussoun's beautiful elder sister, described her first ball at Princess Chevikiar's. Her parents told her not to go near the King. But that was not counting on the King with a honed eye for beauty. He manoeuvred to be the last with her at a Musical Chairs game. Result: she had to dance with him. The Queen had not yet appeared, but Tata described how gorgeous she looked as she descended the stairs. There were no Paris models, but the local dressmakers were well

Prince Abbas Halim with Aunt Emine Tugay

up to the task. The jewels, many from Cartier or Van Cleef & Arpels and others from our local jewellers, Horowitz, Kramer, etc. were truly magnificent. Only Harry Winston could have equalled them in size!

By June, the war in North Africa was going badly for the British. The Germans took Marsa Matruh on June 29th. "The Americans living next to us are said to have left. The Jews also. [Granny's landlord, Mizrahi Pasha, was Jewish]. They say that Ades and Benzion (large Jewish-owned department stores) are selling with 30% rebate to liquidate everything and that the government has stopped payments by the banks. Panic. British HQ has been moved to the Sudan. Lampson has left or is about to leave."

July 2nd. Sebastopol is said to have fallen and the Germans are in front of Alexandria; reports of a great battle in the desert between El Alamein and the depression of Kattara. Next day, Nahas had a 4-hour interview with Lampson, then he was received by the King as was Lampson. The King was in a critical, delicate situation. He was only 22 years old with no devoted friends or advisors, and the antagonist is Great Britain! Taking this into account, he managed surprisingly well during the war years.

In July, Alexandria was bombed. The newspapers reported massive preventive arrests, military tribunals and authority given to the *moudirs* (governors) to rule according to their conscience. Our army dispersed in the provinces, the planes requisitioned, and the defence of Cairo assured by the New Zealanders.

On a lighter note, Mummy took us to tea at the Toussouns, where the King and Queen were present with their two little daughters. We played games, then the King wanted to hear us speak German. I was so shy I could barely talk. To my surprise, he was blond with blue eyes. In photographs, he seemed to have dark hair and dark eyes.

Dad was sent into house arrest on August 3rd and went to see his mother

Nevine

before leaving. Prince Farouk of Turkey and Taher Pasha, one of our cousins, were joining him. "Nahas said he'd managed to prevent them being sent to South Africa...somebody must have signed the document. Some say it was the King, some Nahas, in his position as Military Governor. Seems the lodgings are very comfortable and they are allowed personal servants...but even a golden cage is still a cage."

Three days later, the Queen visited Granny: "Very open and frank..the King said that this was the second blow he had received after that of February 4th..the King did not sign the imprisonment document."

Churchill paid a visit to Egypt, but "in the newspaper photographs not a single Egyptian was present. He was received by Lampson, then he is seen with Smuts, Casey and the generals...Auchinleck, Ritchie fired, Alexander of Dunkirk and Burma replaces Auchinleck. A certain Montgomery replaces Ritchie...gave orders that germanophiles and propagandists should be treated with no consideration and interned as they were in England."

On the occasion of the Queen's 21st birthday, there was a big ball at Roukn Farouk (Farouk's Corner). "We celebrate whatever we can."

The Queen visited Granny again on October 21st as did Queen Nazli on October 30th. She had visits from other members of the Family. Crown Prince Mohamed Ali was a great friend as was Prince Youssef Kemal. Through these visitors and especially through my mother, Granny had a very good idea of what was going on. The newspapers were unreliable as they were full of propaganda. For war news, she had Radio London and Radio Berlin. Granny may have been pro-Axis, but she was no fool and would no more swallow Germany's lies than she would those of the Allies.

On November 9th, "am 67 years old today. A respectable age. What happened during all these years? What angles were softened, how much have wisdom and indulgence progressed?"

At the death of her daughter from diabetes, just a few months before the discovery of insulin, she was heartbroken. When I was born, some of that love was transferred to me. She was very religious, but never discussed her faith. She had no alcohol or pork in the house, but she knew that her son and daughter-in-law drank and probably ate ham, but not suckling pig! She had taught us the two most important Moslem prayers, but went no further.

She sent us to visit the mosques of Cairo, the Egyptian Museum, the Giza and Sakkarah Pyramids with Ulla, Miss Ursula Johannsen, her lady companion, a German from Lithuania. Ulla was the single most loyal person I've ever met. She never had a life of her own, but was a willing slave to Granny. She'd been a refugee and was terribly grateful to Granny and her sister, our Great Aunt Bedia, for rescuing her from a grim destiny. She loved us all and considered herself a member of the family, but a most respectful member. We children were quite good with her, because behind her was Granny, and we were terrified of Granny, who to use a vulgar expression was "a very tough cookie", but a just one. Her justice could seem overdone at times as when she refused to speak to Toppy, our housekeeper, for months because she had not sent Granny her condolences on the death of Aunt Bedia. Poor Toppy considered herself much to "lowly" to send condolences to the *Princesa Kebira*, the "Great Princess."

Granny was the main pillar of our existence and Ulla looked after us whenever one of our governesses disappeared. She also took us to pay visits at Bairam to our aunts and great-aunts: Princess Nimet Muchtar, the sister of King Fouad and Princess Chevikiar, his first wife. We ran into Aunt Emine Toussoun, Mahiveche and Fatma Toussoun, Prince Mohamed Ali, the Crown Prince, Prince Youssef Kemal, Princess Emine Fazil, Aunt Zenab, Madame Hussein Sirry, the Queen's aunt and wife of the sometime Prime Minister.

On September 9th, 1943, Italy surrendered to the Allied Forces. Strangely,

Princess Mahiveche Toussoun

I make no comment on all this. I was much too interested in the important people visiting Granny, like Prince and Princess Abdel Moneim. She was Nesleshah Sultan, daughter of Prince Farouk with whom my father was interned, and much younger than her husband. She was sensationally beautiful and a darling. When I tried to kiss her hand, she said "No, not that, never." She had two gorgeous sisters, who were also married to Egyptian princes: Hanzade, wife of Uncle Mohamed Ali Ibrahim (Dad's first cousin) and Nedjla, wife of Uncle Amr Ibrahim, his brother.

Granny's other visitors were Aunt Shehira and her sister Aunt Malek, Mummy's first cousins. "They are both jolly nice, only Aunt Malek is not very happy as she has had a row with her husband and wants to divorce, I think." She certainly did want to divorce, as her husband, Mohamed Hamada, was having a well-publicised affair with Queen Nazli. To makes things nice and cozy, Aunt Shehira was married to Queen Nazli's brother, Hussein Sabry Pasha.

The King's eldest daughter, Princess Ferial, was four on November 17th. There was a party for poor children in the Palace gardens, where they could walk around, receive food and clothes. "It is a particular trait of the King's to invite the poor to his special parties."

With the arrival of Montgomery, the 8th Army was whipped into shape. Churchill on a visit to Montgomery's headquarters at Borg-el-Arab wrote: "Everybody said what a change there was since Montgomery had taken command. I could feel the truth of this with joy and comfort."

From that time on, the war began to go badly for the Axis. Rommel was turned back at El Alamein and Churchill says in *The Hinge of Fate*: "It may almost be said: Before Alamein we never had a victory. After Alamein we never had a defeat." Of course, this was an enormous over-simplification.

We began to hear of the horrors of concentration camps and the systematic torture and murder of the Jews. How could a country which had fathered so many great musicians, writers, scientists, artists, philosophers have committed such horrific crimes? And then we had not seen half the ghastly truth.

Egypt is thousands of years old. It is used to every shade of skin pigmentation and all religious cults. Queen Nazli's first Lady-in-Waiting was Madame Cattawi Pasha, wife of a prominent Jew. Jews were heavily involved in financial matters in Egypt. They were treated like everybody else, which is more than can be said of the Jews in the USA not so long ago! Same for black people. When we were in the United States in 1948, my sister boarded a streetcar in Washington D.C. and sat next to a black lady. The ticket collector came up to her and asked if she was American. She said she was not, so he informed her that she could not sit next to a black person in public transportation. She could not understand this and would not move, but was finally obliged to. The black lady smiled all over her face and declared: "Honey, you've made my day."

Daddy was then interned in Sirwa, 200 km from Cairo. One evening coming back from visiting him, the car with my mother and Sambo overturned into a ditch. More frightened than hurt, Mummy scrambled out into the muddy water. Miraculously, an Egyptian army patrol car came along, with a doctor aboard. But Mummy had a nervous breakdown. She had held up wonderfully under the stress of my father's absence, the ensuing complications, financial problems, running a household and guiding the education of four children. She did not take to her bed, but her nerves were pretty well shot and she would give us all hell at the slightest provocation. And her father was very ill. She requested an audience of the King and he promised to do his best to get Daddy out of his enforced seclusion. In her words: "My audience with King Farouk. His incredible kindness, frankness and understanding for one so young, the loneliness."

After Mummy's breakdown, she and Ali, who was so sickly, lived at Granny's

Nesleshah Sultan, Princess Abdel Moneim

Nedjla Sultan, Princess Amr Ibrahim

Hanzade Sultan, Princess Mohamed Ali Ibrahim

for a while. Granny's house was in Maadi, a suburb some twelve km from Cairo. It was like an oasis, the streets bordered with trees, the houses boasting gardens riotous with exotic blooms, but except for the Nile to the west, completely hemmed in by desert. After the last house, the sand began.

Granny's house was not very big, but high-ceilinged and three-storied. It was furnished in almost monastic simplicity. The colours were dull, dark brown, grey, pale blue. Granny's great amusement was to change the furniture around completely every now and then. Her bedroom was too cold or too sunny, the living room too draughty, so everything was moved. It must have driven Ulla and the servants crazy. When I would arrive, she'd wait impatiently for my reaction. This, of course, was in later years. But her real fun was organising the cellar for the summer months. It was beautifully whitewashed with rooms and corridors galore. She would install beds, sofas and chairs and once the weather became unbearable, she lived there. It had one horrendous drawback: no loo! Most summers, she eventually went to Alexandria, to a house lent her by her cousin, Behia, the wife of Aziz Pasha Izzet. Aunt Behia was also the sister of my maternal grandmother, so her children were first cousins to Mummy and their children our closest relatives. We had no first cousins because our parents had no siblings, except for our cousins from Daddy's half-sister and brother whom we only met much later and never became intimate.

Granny was lecturing us on how badly behaved we were with the servants, compared to Daddy. She was not too happy a great deal of the time, what with Mummy and Ali living there, her son under arrest, and not much money. Daddy came to visit us at Granny's on his way from Sirwa to his new destination, Ayat. Prince Farouk turned up in a separate car with his wife and daughter Nesleshah with her baby. Dad kissed us all, then went up to Mum alone. She smiled the whole time she was so happy.

Totes was living on Grandpa's houseboat, the *dahabeya,* and rarely visited

122

Aziz Pasha Izzet

his mother in Maadi. He did come to see us in Koubbeh at times and took us for a drive in his Fiat Topolino.

We spent those winters in Koubbeh, being taught by Frau Anni and looked after by Linda. Mummy and Ali finally returned and we were happy to be together again. Daddy was allowed out once to see the occulist and managed to stay a few days. Early July, after our exams, we went to Alexandria to stay with Grandpa.

Mummy came and went between Cairo and Alexandria. We spent the mornings at the beach and the afternoons at Granny's and the Izzets.

The following winter, we gave up the house in Koubbeh Gardens and rented Aunt Zenab's former house in Maadi, just behind Granny's. We were still very pro-German and in my diary I note that none of the pro-German contingent had yet changed sides. The Germans had been kicked out of Africa and the war in Europe was not going well for them, but we were still faithful. We knew little about the concentration camps and any nasty rumours were treated as enemy propaganda. Of course, the British did everything possible to annoy the Egyptians and were incredibly unpleasant to say the least. The troops were the problem, especially the Australians and New Zealanders. They were stationed in Maadi and nobody dared go out at night because of drunken soldiers roaming the streets who beat up men and raped women. There is no mention of this by Lampson or Montgomery. Nor of the cordial relations the King had with President Roosevelt. There is a shot of them on board a warship, the King lighting the President's cigarette and laughing with him.

When Grandpa Yeghen died, the British Ambassador permitted Daddy to attend the funeral, provided there were no street demonstrations from his Labour Party or general followers.

***

At the end of the war, Cairo was a curious place, full of Americans who were fêted, fawned upon and generally admired. Considering that most of us had been pro-German, if not pro-Nazi, the sudden switch was extraordinary. This included my parents. Daddy was finally released from Ayat, we got Garden City back from Mr. Kirk and all was well.

We were at home at last. Mummy redecorated our rooms, had the garden landscaped and gave me the responsibility for overseeing the planting of flowers, bushes and grass. The gardener was a plump young man called Moursi, who was extremely lazy and delegated his small army of gardener boys to do all the hard work. The poor boys were hopeless at planting and I would descend on Moursi and insist he did the work properly. He loved me!

Mummy gave each of us a plot to tend. Ulvia and Ali had vegetable gardens, I had a rose garden where I worked diligently. The other two did little gardening and a great deal of eating; they happily ate raw peas and beans and unhappily caught typhoid fever. Ali was very ill and nearly died, but Ulvia weathered it better and faster. Typhoid was very dangerous then, a neighbour's son had just died of it. It was also contagious. My mother installed me downstairs in the library. I was looked after by Mummy's great friend, Indji Lenos, called Bits, who'd played tennis in international tournaments, representing both Egypt and Greece. She was just back from Greece where she'd spent the War, an experience she would not talk about. With her, I went to the Guezira Sporting Club and mingled with grown-ups.

The Guezira Sporting Club started as the Khedivial Club for British administrators in Egypt. It had four polo grounds, two racecourses, an 18-hole golf course, squash and tennis courts and croquet lawns. It was well-run with beautiful gardens.

Our favourite meeting point was the Lido. As you walked in, up a few stairs, the men's changing rooms and bar were on the right and the women's on the left, with no bar. Tables and chairs on a large terrace gave onto the swimming pool. Sooner or later, you met everybody and it was a more convenient way of planning our activities than telephoning, as we were rarely at home.

Gottfried von Cramm, the German tennis champion showed up after the War. He was a great friend of my parents, charming and so handsome with his golden hair. He was also a perfect gentleman, on and off the court, and not a Nazi. Years later, I saw him at Roland Garros with wife Barbara Hutton sitting in the loge next to ours. It seems Barbara used to say that the most magical sound in the world was the sound of ice cubes in a glass of Scotch. We all agreed.

Daddy as President of the Egyptian Lawn Tennis Association and Mummy as Vice-President knew all the famous players of the day, and we met them too—the French Four Musketeers: Cochet, Lacoste, Borotra and Brugnon, then Simone Matthieu, very active in the French Résistance, Budge Patty, Jaroslav Drobny (he was a Yugoslav refugee who was a naturalised Egyptian and played for Egypt), Nelly Landry, Frank Parker, Tony Mottram, etc.

Every year, at the end of the International Tennis Tournaments of Cairo and Alexandria, my parents gave a ball in Garden City. I was finally allowed to attend when I was sixteen. "My evening dress arrived…and when I tried it on it was less fattening than I had previously thought. I hope I will not look too plump and stupid–young girl on the night. If there is something I loathe, it is the horrid stupidity of the *jeune fille*, fat, white and pretty and really awfully silly-looking."

I spent most of my teens in the throes of horrendous crushes. Thankfully, I was much too shy to approach the objects of my affection. This time Philippe Washer, a handsome Belgian tennis player, was at the ball and even asked me to dance. He called me *Mademoiselle Abbas Halim* and we danced cheek to cheek. Heaven! It was Leap Year and for the first dance, the ladies had to invite the gentlemen to dance. I chose Victor Simeika, one of my parents' oldest friends and one of the few I knew reasonably well. He never let me forget that he was the chosen one at my first ball. He died only a few years ago, well over ninety, the perfect "man about town", world traveller, polo player, married several times to beautiful women, always full of enthusiasm and ready for any escapade. I was less lucky in my dinner partner, accosted by somebody I called the Bore who talked of nothing but history, geography and social standards. I even had to give him a dance after dinner, but then I escaped and danced till I could scarcely see straight, with the Spanish, Italian and Dutch ministers, with Messrs. Geehland and Peten, Belgian tennis players, Pierre Tawil and Constantin Camara, friends of my parents. I danced with lots I don't remember. I ended by telling their fortunes, by the lines in their hands. "When Philippe Washer, who is awfully conceited, left, he said he hoped to have his told next time. At 4 a.m. I went upstairs."

I remember two other parties worth mentioning. One was at Mr. and Mrs. Pinkney Tuck's. He was the American Minister and they were great friends of my parents. Two of my school friends were there, Cyril Cacace and Van Rechteren. Cyril was tall, blond and very good looking but I did not have a crush on him. In fact, we quarrelled a lot. At the party, we had a terrific fight because I danced with Cherif Zulfikar, the Queen's brother, and did not wait for Cyril who had gone off to find Van.

The second party was at Edna and Bobby Khayatt's. They had a lovely house in Guezira called Villa Yildiz with a beautiful garden, which has now made way for "a large US Embassy housing unit." Cherif was there again and we danced a lot together and had a terrific time. Cherif was very handsome and an extremely nice boy. Daddy and Mummy even waited for me to finish the dance to take me home. Cherif later had polio and thanks to his father's stubborn dedication, he was able to move again and regained much of his mobility. But, of course, he could no longer practice the sports he loved.

There was also Nevine Sirry's wedding to Ismaïl Mazloum. She was the daughter of the occasional Prime Minister, Hussein Sirry. Aunt Zenab, Princess Zenab Hilmi, and her husband, Seyfullah Yousry Pasha took me to the party. He was a polo player and golfer and also the First Undersecretary of State for Foreign Affairs and Egyptian Minister in Washington and Berlin under King Fouad. I remember the wedding because it was the first time I saw Tahia Carioca dance. Her grace and beauty were a revelation.

Totes appeared occasionally. When we moved to Koubbeh, he went to live on Grandpa's *dahabeya* (houseboat). He was on pretty bad terms with his mother and with Dad not around to arrange things, we rarely saw him. In Koubbeh, Granny's first cousin, Princess Mahiveche Fazil lived around the corner with her two sons, Djesouli and Ilhami, and their wives, Seldjouk and Rukia. Much later in life, Totes married Seldjouk and she became our much-loved sister-in-law. She was the daughter of a Turkish Imperial prince and Dad's first cousin, Princess Emine Halim. She made Totes so happy, although not for long. "Life is not fair", as JFK is supposed to have said, and in this case it was terribly unfair. They were married in Paris in 1966, whence Totes had literally escaped after the revolution. He worked at Dassault's during the day and did translations at night to make ends meet. They moved to Monte Carlo in 1974 where Totes had a good job and could finally relax a little. She developed breast cancer. He went through hell and back until she died. He looked after her and followed up every rumour of a cure. There was a medicine in the U.S. called Interferon which seemed promising. He had Ali in Washington ask an old friend of ours, Bill Amorosa, a cancer specialist if he could obtain the medicine. But it was too early to use on human beings. Seldjouk died on May 11, 1980. Totes told me he'd never thought he could love somebody as much as he loved Seldjouk. It took him years to recover.

Totes and Seldjouk on their wedding day in Paris

***

Our servants played an important role in our lives. Most of them had been in the family for years, some since they were children. There was Abdu, my father's valet whose voice on the phone sounded exactly like Dad's. He was a thin, rather taciturn Sudanese, who drank like a fish. He drank *taffia*, a ghastly liquor made up of nearly pure alcohol. My father tried to wean him off the stuff, with decent Scotch or brandy, but with no success. He only drank in the evening when off duty. Next we had Mohamed Abdel Meguid, the handy man, who later went up in life to become assistant butler; *Am* Ismaïl, the old ironer who had been to Paris with Grandpa and never forgot it; Inayet the Circassian housekeeper, named "Toppy" and our particular pet, was great at a sick bed; Sambo, the chauffeur, whom we all adored as he had such a sweet round black face, but who would not tolerate bad behaviour. Ghattas, the other chauffeur, was a Copt who prided himself on speaking English. And of course the cook, Osta Mohamed. He arrived by taxi every morning with his purchases, a good-looking man, always very elegant in suit and tie. Lastly, the *bawab* (doorman), a huge Nubian called Ali. He sat in a niche dressed in a spotless white *galabeya* with an equally spotless white turban magnificently wound around his head.

These servants did not change. But the kitchen and garden boys, the maids and under butlers came and went in rapid succession, but not nearly as rapidly as the governesses. We prided ourselves on having chased out fifteen to twenty in the course of six or seven years. We were the terrors of the governesses of Cairo. Whenever my mother applied to an agency for a new one, the agency had a hard time finding another victim. We had French, English, Italian, Greek, Russian, German and Swiss governesses.

In rich Western countries, where there are rarely any "servants" as the most

Prince Abbas Halim with faithful retainers, in the garden at Schutz 1967:
(standing from left) Haroun and Sambo, (sitting from left) Hassoun and Abdu

menial jobs have pompous titles, the employer treats them with great caution. Our servants were servants, but most of them had grown up with our parents and were considered members of the family. When they needed a loan, clothes, doctors, help with their children's schools or jobs, they would ask for it. And they were never disappointed. In return they did the same for us. After the revolution, Sambo's sons lent us money when we were broke. Some refused to take their salaries and said they could wait until times were better. But it took a long time for things to get better.

* * *

We were taught at home, I until the age of fifteen, Ulvia until nearly twelve, and Ali until about ten. We had a marvellous Austrian teacher called Frau Anni Kemhadjian, who taught all subjects in German. Frau Anni was from Salzburg, married to an Armenian journalist and very pro-Axis during the war. She was the only one we respected in the governess/teacher category. She did not live with us and was not expected to discipline us outside school hours. This lasted for about four years. She suffered a great loss not long after she came to us: her little daughter became ill and died. The light went out of Frau Anni's eyes for many months. Then she had to leave us as she was expecting a baby and we were delighted for her.

We still had a governess. Linda was engaged to a German POW, whom she visited in Fayed, a concentration camp near the Suez Canal. When she received permission to visit him or had to absent herself for some reason, Mme Shoukry, a friend of Mummy's who also lived in Koubbeh, looked after us. She was a German married to an Egyptian and also pro-Axis. We were very fond of her as she was always full of fun and did not bother much with discipline. We went to Granny's nearly every afternoon, especially when Mum was living

132

there, so it was not too onerous a job. We also went shopping to all the big department stores: Chemla, Sednaoui, Cicurel and Orosdi-Back. The shops carried merchandise of excellent quality and all the saleswomen spoke good French. Today, only bad English is spoken, as most of the saleswomen who were Italian, Jewish or Greek, left after the revolution.

Frau Anni persuaded my mother to send us to school, especially as I wanted to go on to university and would need a diploma from a high school. We were all enrolled in the English School in Heliopolis. The headmaster was D.H. Whiting, whose death was mentioned in the Daily Telegraph many years later, citing his distinguished career. Another MI6? Spy or not, he was an excellent headmaster, with a staff almost entirely British, except for the teachers of French and Arabic.

At one point, we were learning five languages at the same time: German, English, French, Arabic and Turkish. In Turkish and Arabic, we had private lessons. Our Turkish teacher, Süreya Bey Tarbagatay, was a kindly man who suffered our bad behaviour with true stoicism. The poor man probably needed the job. I asked him about the Great Family Quarrel, and he explained that King Fouad had demoted all princes and princesses not directly related to the sovereign to the unknown titles of nabil and nabila. This title existed nowhere outside Egypt and was generally ignored except on official occasions. It put the entire Family against him; not surprising, as it brought all the former princes and princesses down a very big peg!

For Arabic, we first had a lovely lady who was quite willing to discuss the latest films we'd seen, in English. She did not last long and was replaced by an Arabic scholar. A disaster. He only spoke classical Arabic and we only spoke the lower kitchen variety. From this experience I remember the beginning of a fairy tale, which we had to learn by heart and went: "In the olden days, there was a prince from amongst the Persian princes…"

At first, Mummy insisted on sending us to school by car with Sambo, but we were the butt of nasty remarks from our fellow students. We pleaded desperately to take the bus and finally she agreed, provided the bus stopped at our gate.

I hated school, maths and science. I'd been very good at maths with Frau Anni, but could make neither head nor tail of what Mr. Horrocks taught us. He was a brilliant man incapable of explaining these subjects to a room full of half-wits. Exactly two girls could pass a test, one of them having doubled her class. The other was Lillian Besso, who became a great friend of mine. And not because she helped me with my maths! Another friend was Helen Constantinidis.

As for boys, I had intense, secret crushes on one or another during my three school years. I was absolutely terrified of them and could never get out one intelligent sentence in their presence. Once at a party at Lillian's, we played the bottle game and one of the boys, a very good looking one called Isaac Boss, kissed me on the mouth. I carried around this memory as if it were a supreme experience and at one point was worried that I might be pregnant.

In spite of maths, I was either first or second in class. My perpetual rival was Susan Wilson, a very nice girl as long as she did not beat me. Students were divided into Houses, on the girls' side they were Windsor, Kent, Gloucester and York and on the boys' side Drake, Frobisher, Raleigh, Grenville. I was in Windsor and in my last year I should have been named Head of Windsor, but Mummy would not allow me to participate in any sports due to my "heart murmur." Sports were of prime importance and the House Captain had to organise, encourage and take part. I did my best to show interest and Helen, an excellent hockey player, made me practice behind Mummy's back, so I might have a hands-on knowledge of the sport. This was to no avail. One of our House mates, Annie Schock, was champion of Egypt in the 100 m, and as such she became

Head of Windsor. Her scholastic abilities were nil, so the pill I had to swallow was more bitter. I go on about it in my diary: "In big break, we had a Windsor hockey practice. It went frightfully, with that fool Annie shouting at the girls as if they were fools or servants. I feel more and more humiliated every time I see what a rotten House Captain she is. I could have been a good deal better than that, games or no games."

"Arabic was a bore as usual and so was French. The kind of French we do is enough to send us good ones to sleep and tuck us up for the night. We are reading the most horribly stupid and dull short stories by Guy de Maupassant, most of them without any point or meaning whatsoever. You struggle through the beastly story, come to the end, finding absolutely nothing worth your trouble and remain with a stupid look of amazement and disappointment on your face."

The school sometimes sent us on excursions and one day we visited the House of Parliament, "a really beautiful building. The waiting room is long and decorated in the ancient Egyptian style. The Hall itself has the Throne at one end on a platform, benches forming a circle around the room and balconies lining the sides. The Queen's balcony is just opposite the Throne and covered with a green velvet drapery, on which a gold crown is incrested."

In April 1948, our last year at school, Mum gave away the sports prizes. "Everybody asked if it was my mother presenting them and this morning the Head pointed out certain etiquette towards Her Highness. I took a photo as she was handing one to Marke Zervudachi." Marke was Head Boy and received several prizes. As he came up once more, Mum laughed and said: "You again!" He and his elder brother, Nolly, have remained our great friends ever since.

Marke became very enthusiastic about boxing although his parents were strongly opposed to it. Dad would sometimes call Marke into his study, after he'd brought Ulvia home from some social event, to discuss boxing. Bersolesi, known as "Battling Vic" in his heyday would be present as a real live boxer.

On June 14th, "the Head read out the Prize winners. When he read out that Susan had carried off, besides Scripture, Latin, History, the Form Prize and the Horan and English Prize, I nearly fainted with horror and disbelief. The English Prize, which I had almost known mine, she had to have and the Form Prize, which I had stood an excellent chance of getting, she had to receive also…Later, I had a complete breakdown…and cried." In fact, I was second "in everything I was good at."

But on July 1st, the final reports arrived and "mine was simply smashing. I have never had such a good one, even when I came first instead of second in the Year and in English and History. I was terribly glad it was good, for as I came only second, I was afraid they would say I was losing my grip. It gives me a little hope for better results than I have hitherto dared to hope for, in the S.C. Exams."

I ran into our English teacher, Mrs. Horrocks, wife of our maths/science teacher, but much more human. She asked me how I'd liked my prize and was very sorry that I had not got the Horan Prize, but when she added it all up, Susan came first. She thought I should come back to get a Higher School Certificate. I told her I would have loved to, but had decided to study music.

I was studying Mozart's 5th Sonata, Schumann's Arabesque, Chopin's Mazurka No. 17, as well as scales and exercises of course. I cannot pretend that I was wildly enthusiastic about playing the piano and I did not have the dedication of a true musician. Still there was a magical moment when Madame Gina Bachauer taught me. With her, both my interpretation and my skill improved impressively. She was a great pianist and after the war she returned to her concert playing all over the world. And I sank into mediocrity!

Just before the end of the war, Mummy bought a house in Alexandria at Schutz tram station. The localities were named after the tram stations from

Ramleh Station, the main station in downtown Alex, to Victoria, where Victoria College was located. Our new house belonged to a Swiss couple, Mr. and Mrs. Alfred Scurmann, and hence was in good condition with a lovely garden. We now had our own home and did not have to go to Granny's or Grandpa's every summer. We rather liked this as we were no longer subject to close scrutiny by Granny and suspicious glances from Grandpa. When Daddy got out of prison, he bred chickens, ducks, pigeons and rabbits. He also built a large aviary, full of multi-coloured birds. For the ducks, he had little ponds and waterways built among flowering bushes at the back of the house. In front was a large pond full of goldfish. We loved the baby ducks and chicken. Later, he bought us two Persian kittens, which were so gorgeous we went gaga. But they were very delicate and both died, suffocating from swallowing their own hair. It was a major tragedy. Our next cat was extremely unattractive, saved by Ulvia from drowning by the gardener. Ali and I thought it was a pity he survived, as he was rather nasty. Ulvia has been rescuing animals all her life and today we have a ghastly collection of stray cats in the garden in Schutz.

Ulvia was my antithesis. Where I was conscientious and careful, she was wild. She worked very hard at times, but rarely finished anything. Having fun was her priority in life. My father was not much help as she could twist him around her finger. After our parents separated, discipline went out the window.

***

During the summer of 1947, before the coming upheavals, we travelled to Europe. Mummy had sold the house in Brunoy, badly damaged during the war, and with this windfall we sailed from Alexandria on a Greek ship called *Attiki*. Our cousins, Bahia and Aleya Izzet, were also on board with their father, Abdullah Izzet, Mummy's first cousin. We met his new wife Maria, called Aicha

Villa Montfleurie, Schutz, Alexandria

when she became a Moslem, a Bulgarian singer Uncle had met in a nightclub. She was great fun and we adopted her, mostly because the Izzet family were horrified by the marriage and would have nothing to do with her. We were very fond of Uncle and she made him happy, so what the hell!

On board were also Count and Countess Charles de Zogheb, Charlie and Frieda, who were very good company and treated us youngsters like members of the human race and not something to be avoided at all costs. After all, Bahia and I were eighteen and seventeen respectively, and not easily forgotten. The younger ones made more noise, but we were *there*. As a bit of name-throwing gossip, the Zogheb's eldest daughter later married and divorced Paul Anka.

The boat sailed via Piraeus and Naples to Marseilles, where we separated from our friends and from Ulvia and Ali. Dad took them to Switzerland to Châlet Marie José in Gstaad for the summer, thanks to the introduction Mum had obtained from the American Ambassador Pinkney Tuck. The "children" as I condescendingly called Ulvia and Ali were furious at being abandoned in the Alps. Ali, a lazy little pest, was especially annoyed because of all the physical exercise he had to endure. Ulvia was the sporty type and a friendly little soul who got on with everybody and soon adapted to her surroundings.

I was being treated almost as a grown-up. François, the French chauffeur we had hired, drove Mum, Bits and me to Paris in the Buick we had brought over on the ship. We stayed at the Hotel California in Rue de Berri. It was very soon after the war and there was still bread rationing and even tourists had to get *tickets de pain*. The bread was pretty awful too. But Paris was again the City of Light, grateful not to have been destroyed by Hitler's orders. Later I saw the film made from Larry Collins and Dominique Lapierre's bestseller *Is Paris burning?* and I realised how dreadful a loss it would have been.

When Dad arrived from Switzerland, we moved to Deauville and my snobbish little heart was full. We found Uncle Saïd Toussoun there with his gloriously beautiful wife Mahiveche and his sister Aunt Emina. He had horses racing that season and owned the *Harras de la Barberie* nearby. When he later married my best friend Nanou, she invited me there for a weekend. It was a lovely spot, with stables of course and a private racecourse. The main house was on one floor and very home-like. There was a smaller house for the children: two sons, Hussein and Hassan, and a daughter Nesrine from his first wife and Aziz who was Nanou's son.

Normandy is a symphony in green, with characteristic buildings beautifully blending into the landscape. Later, Saïd sold the *Harras* to Alain and Gérard Wertheimer.

Another cousin of my parents, Princess Zenab and her husband Seifullah Pasha Yousry, who had taken me to Nevine Sirry's wedding, were at the Golf Hotel. He a very enthusiastic golfer. Aunt Zenab said his wish was to die on the golf course, and that is exactly what he did.

My parents, Bits and I stayed at the Hotel Normandie, built like a huge chalet. The bedrooms were decorated in chintz: curtains, walls, bedcovers, chair covers. My room was blue and white chintz. The hotel was near the beach, the Casino, the best restaurants and shops, we could go almost anywhere on foot.

Not surprisingly, the Royal Golf Hotel was surrounded by an 18-hole golf course. The race track was not far. Deauville hosted golf tournaments, horse races, vintage car competitions, fashion shows and exhibitions of all kinds.

During the day, I often went cycling around the countryside. At first Bits came with me, but after a while she got bored. Then one memorable day, wearing a red blouse, cycling in a new direction, I excited the passion of a bull in a neighbouring field. There was a solid fence between us, but I was not about to put my fate to the test and rode as fast as I could towards town. Unfortunately, I almost upset Uncle Saïd as he was coming out of the stables.

Baron de Nexon, Aunt Zenab Helmi, Said Toussoun, Mum, Billie York
Deauville 1947

He wanted to know why I was in such a hurry and I had to explain. He laughed uproariously and told the story to all my other relatives to my intense mortification.

Not one of my fond relations thought to introduce me to people my age. It's true they were very scarce. In fact, I only noticed one, blond and handsome, the son of an English trainer. We eyed each other from afar, but never even said hello. I was underage and not allowed into the gambling rooms at the Casino, but one evening there was a gala dinner there and Bits and I were invited by my parents. Of course, there were the Toussouns, the Yousrys, an English tennis player, Billie Yorke, and the Baron de Nexon of Guerlain. The ladies wore fabulous dresses and even more fabulous jewels.

Bits and I returned to Paris for a while with Mummy, who had herself fitted out for gorgeous evening dresses at Balmain and Jean Desses, where I discovered the world of *haute couture*. We went on an expedition to Versailles in the Buick with François. Bits and I also visited the Louvre Museum, the Carnavalet Museum and had most of our meals in cafés on the Champs Elysées. I was even allowed to drink a beer once in a while.

Dad went to Switzerland to fetch the "children." Edmond Soussa met him in Geneva and Ulvia and Ali were thoroughly spoiled by the two men. They specifically ate like pigs. And were not sick.

We returned to Egypt on the *Pace*, an Italian ship, not much better than the *Attiki*, but none of the pre-war liners were yet ready to resume de luxe passenger service. There were added complications, as there was a cholera epidemic in Egypt. We had to be vaccinated in Marseilles before boarding and for some reason our urine analysed. The poor Egyptian Consul in Marseilles was running around town trying to get everything ready in time for our departure. I don't think he ever lived down the urine samples.

Now that we had the house in Alexandria, we were no longer dependent on Granny or Grandpa. We also had a cabin at Sidi Bishr No. 2, which was the *in* beach. All our friends and cousins had cabins there or shared them. They were pretty spartan. Outside, wooden benches with cushions were fitted around the walls, and inside we put up plastic curtains to ensure some privacy to change. There was no running water or electricity. You showered under the public shower and brought your own lamps if you intended to stay late. Remaining after sunset was frowned upon by our parents and the beach guards, but we could have an occasional evening party, provided we had permission.

Our special friends were the Izzets and the three Zakis: Tata (who married my husband before me), Tarek the only good looking boy we knew and all fell in love with, and finally Nawal, called Nanou, who was my special friend. She married Uncle Saïd Toussoun many years later and that's when we stopped with the "uncle" bit. We met at the beach in the morning and generally went to the Izzets' house in the afternoon. Various other friends joined us there: Boubi El Sayed, Aleya Moharrem, and the children of the house, Leila and Aziz. Leila was the same age as Ali and Aziz was a baby. Leila, a tomboy like Ulvia, rode, swam and generally engaged in some sporting activity. She had a great talent for drawing, mostly animals, and with time developed into a gifted painter.

The San Stefano house of our Aunt Behia and her husband, Aziz Pasha Izzet, was a wonderful place, with many rooms, stairways and mysterious corridors. A great many people lived there, with an enormous staff. There was even a live-in Arabic teacher, whom we all loved as she was so pretty and very nice to us. The house had been recently renovated, but that had not changed its appeal. It was difficult to explore the house, if you ventured too far, you inevitably

Nevine with Prince Abbas Halim in Sidi Bishr

came face to face with a maid, a valet, a doctor, a nurse, or an aunt. One subject of great interest was the number of medicines to be found on the dining room table. Instead of silver candlesticks, the entire middle section of the table was covered with boxes, bottles and jars of medicines. We were very rarely invited to join our Great Aunt for a meal, but once in a while we would peak into the dining room to check on the medicines. They were ever more numerous. They must have been great because my Aunt and Uncle lived to well past 90!

Alexandria was a clean, well-run town, more so than Cairo, because of the huge foreign communities, mainly Greek, Italian and Jews of various nationalities. They made fortunes in cotton and wood, built hospitals, schools, social clubs and, of course, private houses with beautiful gardens. They developed entire sections of town, such as Smouha with a racecourse and the Antoniadis Gardens with a small zoo. Schools were run by Catholic Mères, Soeurs, Frères and Jesuits; there were also English and German schools. Many foreigners considered themselves partially Egyptian, as was evident at the time of the revolution. They owned land, built "country houses", again surrounded by beautiful gardens. Alexandria gardeners were renowned for their skill. These days Alexandria may be looking up again, thanks to the new library, the Bibliotheca Alexandrina, the new hotels and the beautiful new Corniche.

They were carefree summers and we did enjoy them. Our house in Schutz was much smaller than Garden City and not nearly as grand. But we loved it too, if not with the same devotion. The Schutz house was on a slight elevation amid flowering bushes and enormous trees, which effectively screened it from our neighbours. Neighbours were few and far between. Now, most of the surrounding houses and gardens have given place to high-rises. If it were not for the trees, the place would be uninhabitable. Daddy loved to garden and soon made this one a thing of beauty: two winding paths led from the garden entrance to the steps leading up to the front door. At every turn there were

Princess Nawal Toussoun

arches covered with honeysuckle or bougainvilliers and the scent of the magnolia blossoms was intoxicating.

* * *

The real world was waiting with a vengeance. Jews had been slowly infiltrating Palestine, and in 1882, they founded the first agricultural colony near Jaffa. Clandestine immigration, subsidised by the Jewish Colonial Bank and the National Jewish Fund enabled these colonies to grow, funding the purchase of land at very low prices. Tel Aviv was founded near Jaffa in 1909. In 1914, the Jewish population was 100,000. The Balfour declaration in 1917, agreeing to a Jewish homeland in Palestine as long as it did not prejudice Arab rights, was a piece of double-talk. London was multiplying its promises to the Arabs to have them revolt against the Ottomans. With Hitler coming to power in 1933, the number of Jews in Palestine in 1935 grew to 335,000. A general rebellion by the Arabs in 1936 forced the British to limit Jewish immigration to 75,000 for a period of five years, and when the Arabs continued to protest, they stopped it almost completely in 1940. The Irgun, a clandestine group of terrorists, which had separated itself from the Haganah (the future Israeli Army) attacked the Arabs and the British army. The Stern gang, another terrorist group joined the Irgun, headed then by Menahem Begin, future Prime Minister of Israel, and by 1945 so did the Haganah. Britain, overwhelmed, handed the problem over to the United Nations. The British Mandate ended on May 14th 1948 and the same day, Ben Gurion declared the State of Israel.

On May 15th 1948, the armies of Egypt, Transjordan, Syria, Iraq and Lebanon invaded the regions occupied by the Jews. At first all went well for the Arabs, however, after a truce (11th June-9th July) arranged by Count Bernadotte, the UN mediator, the Jews organised themselves and thoroughly

147

trounced all the Arabs. Egypt was the first to ask for an armistice. As usual, the Arabs had flung themselves any old how into the fray. They were neither properly armed nor properly led and the truce was their undoing.

Meanwhile, the King had been making stupid personal and political mistakes. He seemed to have changed greatly at the end of the war. He declared he was descended from the Prophet and had the right to the title of Sherif. Then he got himself involved in supplying the army with defective weapons. His group of Syrio-Lebanese sycophants were the guilty ones in all likelihood, but his name was mentioned and his popularity reached a new low. He was on bad terms with most of the princes, especially with my father, who did not hide the fact that he thought the King was making dangerous errors in judgement. The King accused my father of supplying the defective weapons and had him investigated, but Dad had dealt with a prestigious Swiss firm called Oerlikon and could prove it.

The Queen, tired of his philandering and his dubious entourage, had moved with her children to another palace and eventually asked for a divorce. Granny persisted that the Queen had handled her husband badly, making scenes and trying to make him jealous. Most of us believed that the King was in love with her and did not want a divorce. Yet he refused to give up his circle of friends, which was one of her conditions for a reconciliation. Neither was totally to blame. They married in their teens, both were extremely spoilt, surrounded by "yes" people. At the beginning of their reign, they were idolised. The handsome young King met many beautiful women, some of whom were only too ready to seduce him. Any man must have enormous will power to resist and he obviously had none. The Queen was extremely jealous and while she tried to ignore the more superficial flirtations, his affair with the wife of a cousin was the final drop. The King was very reluctant to divorce her, but she was persistent so he finally agreed to let her go.

Dom João d'Orleans Bragance, Princess Faiza, Prince Nicholas Romanoff,
Princess Fawzia, Bulent Raouf and Princess Fatma Toussoun, 1948

Empress Fawzia was also having problems and a double announcement was made: The King and Queen of Egypt and the Emperor and Empress of Iran had decided to divorce. This was very sad and bad for the King's image, as the Queen was admired and loved. His night-clubbing and womanising were not considered sinful, but he lost a great deal of respect by mixing with unsavoury characters. When he was younger, he had seemed to care about Egypt and to want to be a good ruler. But one forgets that in 1948 he was only 28 years old. Slowly he became fatter and fatter. Where was our beautiful prince? He was also getting bald. Nobody remembered that he had been blond with blue eyes. Now he hid them behind dark glasses and you could never tell what he was thinking or who he was looking at. My father, after the first hopeful years, was thoroughly disillusioned with him. My mother, however, had a soft spot for him. When Daddy had been under house arrest during the war, the King had sent his wife to our house in Koubbeh, to tell her how sorry he was and that he had tried to prevent the imprisonment and had refused to sign the document of internment.

Certainly all the rubbish about not respecting the King was rapidly forgotten when you happened to be in his vicinity. Whatever his faults, there was no doubt that he was the King. I saw him at the Royal Automobile Club where he gambled almost every night. I also saw him at various nightclubs where he was "incognito." Nobody ever forgot who he was.

And he could be very understanding. At his second wedding to Nariman, he and his new queen received members of the Royal Family and the diplomatic corps. After I had made my *temenah* (with your hand you touch the ground, your heart and your head) to the King, I made another one to the Queen and waited for her to give me her hand. Nothing happened and I was getting panicky. I had no intention of bowing again. He noticed, gave me a smile and told her to shake my hand at once. The poor girl seemed scared to

Princess Fatma Toussoun

death. I met her many years later, and found a charming and very well-behaved lady. I don't know who taught her the ropes, but she was an excellent student.

The King was still in power amid a general feeling of unrest. There were rumours he would be assassinated. He ignored them and continued his usual activities with no extra security measures. I think at that point he could still have saved it all, but he certainly misjudged the depth of alienation in the country and perhaps could not be bothered to make an effort. His health was none too good either. He had become much too fat and ate enormous quantities of heavy food. He drank quarts of sugarcane juice which is the most fattening beverage that exists. But he was still full of energy in the evening and stayed up to all hours every night. He no longer had a "home" to go to as he told one of his hostesses who asked him to leave so that all the other guests at her party could go home.

Sadly, it could have turned out differently. A promising boy had changed completely and ruined everything. And today, Egypt is a horrendous mess.

* * *

After our trip to Europe in 1947, on the advice of her Jewish friends, specifically René and Céline Cattawi, and assessing the general political situation in Egypt, Mummy decided to sell the house in Garden City and take all the valuables to the United States. There was another problem we knew nothing about: our parent's marriage was on the rocks. It seems that Daddy, never the most faithful of husbands, was for the first time flaunting his latest conquest, a Syrian lady who had previously been linked to the King. Mummy could take no more and with the political situation as an excuse, she booked a passage for May 1st to the United States.

I sat with Mum in the salon on April 10th. The rules she laid out for our behaviour during her absence were pretty strict. We could do nothing without the agreement and/or presence of Bits, or her sister-in-law, Mrs. Lenos. There was to be no gallivanting about on our own, so any relief we might feel at her departure was wishful thinking. She said she'd arrange for us to pass the summer in a cool place, Maine or California. I was horrified at the idea of losing our beautiful home and never coming back again. There was also the danger of another war with Israel.

I did manage to drive Ulvia to Guezira one day to visit Dad's yacht. We found him there with Victor Simeika, co-owner, and they showed us around. It was small, but everything was neat and shiny and we made them promise to take us on board as soon as they reached Alexandria.

Once Mum left, we saw Dad more often. He told us about all his sporting activities and his interest in social reform. He talked "to some of the 4000 labourers who had gone on strike at the Matossian Cigarette Factory. Today I listened in while he rebuked them for always spoiling what he was trying to do for their own good. They frequently interrupted and Dad listened to anyone who wished to talk very patiently. Terribly interesting, I must say!"

In Egypt, of course, he knew everybody, or rather most people knew him. After all, knowing people is half the battle. He also helped them. When Anwar el Sadat was hunted by the police, he gave him some money and a change of clothes. President Sadat never forgot and when Daddy died he proved it. Sadat, I would like to underline, was one of the very few people who never forgot a helping hand. Most people seem to prefer to bite the hand that helped them.

A word about our supposed *privileges* as members of the Royal Family: one was short number licence plates, Cairo with one or two numbers. Alexandria did not count. When they saw these plates, policemen would salute us. We could also count on a red carpet when we boarded a train. I thought that really great, as the policemen pushed everybody else off the platform as we advanced

153

towards our carriage. We also had the use of a posh waiting room. That was about all we got!

I think none of us realised how terrible this revolution was going to be for us, as well as for so many others. The Royal Family was the first to pay the price, sometimes to cheering from the sidelines. Unfortunately the sidelines, the rich pashas and beys, were next on the list. Then the foreigners, first the rich were nationalised and then after the "Triple and Cowardly War" in 1956, all British and French citizens were sequestrated and given orders to leave the country. The new rulers took a liking to sequestration and soon anybody with money, whether Egyptian or foreign, were deprived of their houses, factories or businesses.

The large Greek, Italian and Jewish communities had people from all walks of life who could no longer make a living as their clients had either lost everything or had left the country. They now had to return to their countries of origin. I met some of them, a maître d'hotel in Athens, another in Rome, and they were miserable. Their compatriots were generally nasty to them as they were competitors on the job market. Not very diplomatically, they kept talking of Egypt and how happy they had been there and how horrid it was in their new surroundings. I met our beloved François, the hairdresser, at Elizabeth Arden's in Milan. He had made good, but he and his wife were miserable. It is difficult to explain what was so enchanting about Egypt then: the easy camaraderie, the fact that if you had serious troubles you'd always find help, the weather, even if too hot or too cold at times, but mostly the sun shone and hope returned.

***

We were off on another adventure: to the United States of America.

The contrast between the feelings America inspires today and the love and admiration we felt for it after the war is difficult to reconcile. We wanted to be as much like them as possible, dress like them, talk like them, live like them. They were not the British, even if they spoke a variant of English, and in spite of their racial problems at home, they behaved very democratically towards all the different peoples they met with abroad. The movies, of course, painted an idyllic picture of the American way of life.

Politics raised its ugly head once the United States decided to take Britain's place in the world. They were not interested in actually ruling another country, but they meant to protect their interests, primarily oil. And they were obsessed with communism. They made enormous mistakes in getting rid of King Farouk and the Shah of Iran, both Britain and America paid a heavy price for this stupidity. America's dislike of royalty goes back to George III, I suppose. They believe royalty is essentially undemocratic, even if Britain is a prime example of a royal democracy. They support republican regimes that steal the aid, give nothing but misery to their people, and not bother to follow America's wishes, for which they received the aid.

On Friday, July 16th, 1948, we embarked on the *Khedive Ismaïl,* destination New York. The trip was to take 15 or 16 days. We were accompanied to Alexandria harbour by Dad, Totes, Ulla (Granny's lady companion), Mrs. Lenos, and our parent's secretaries Mahgoub and Farrag Effendi. Bits was chaperoning us again. The ship left Alexandria at 4 p.m.

That morning, Dad took us to the beach where he taught me the basics of the crawl. We said goodbye to all our Izzet cousins and Uncle Mohamed, had lunch at home and drove to the harbour.

On board, we were soon joined by other young people, whose parents were friends of ours. They were Mohsen and Anwar Wissa and Nimet and Adi

Princess Tawhida Halim in Washington

Wahba. There was also a horrid-looking fellow who stuck to us and cheated at cards.

Our first stop was Naples. We had seen it the year before and considerable progress had been made in its reconstruction. To visit Pompeii, we took a comfortable, new shining bus. On the way we stopped at a shop, where beautiful coral jewellery, tortoise shell cases and toilet articles were exhibited. The year before, Daddy had bought Mum a coral necklace, with several twisted strands ending in a big gold clasp.

Pompei, except for the forum, consisted of ruined stone walls and endless streets. Only adults were allowed in the rooms with pornographic paintings on the walls. Nowadays small children can watch the most ghastly scenes on television, body parts blown up by terrorist attacks, and as for sex, it has no secrets for them any more. More heartbreaking is seeing small children actually living the horror, as their parents, friends and homes are blasted into smithereens.

Next afternoon, we arrived in Genoa. We were all very excited and raced around the ship to get the best view of the approaching city. Later we walked around the harbour and came upon the *Malek Fouad* and spoke to the stewards in Arabic to their astonishment and joy. Egyptians with foreigners are polite but distant, but when they meet another Egyptian away from home, they are so happy they don't know what to do to please you.

We went for a sail in the harbour with an 72-year-old man who had been all around the world and spoke quite good English. He was hale, hearty and full of stories about his travels.

Back on board, we were in time to watch the *Malek Fouad* on her way out. She looked very lovely, with the many tiny lights twinkling merrily.

We remained in Genoa all next day and decided to visit the modern part of the city by trolley car, returning to the port by tram. This was a new and exciting experience because none of us had ever taken a trolley or tram in Egypt. We dined in a restaurant on the top floor of a skyscraper. We'd never seen such a high building before and were entranced by the fabulous view.

When we reached Marseilles, the Wissas and Wahbas left us and we felt lost and lonely. Soon we made friends with two Turkish girls, Daisy and Leila, an elderly American couple we adopted and called Grandpa and Grandma, and Jackie from Texas with her parents. There was also Doc and the Americans Phyllis, Gwen and Barry, so that in no time we had formed a new group.

There was more space now. Bits and I moved into separate luxurious cabins with wonderful bathrooms. We spread our belongings around and were much more comfortable.

On July 30th, the Chief Engineer presented himself to me, saying he was ready to show us the engine room. My! What a beautiful place it was! Clean, everything spotless, huge boilers, condensers, distillers, boards with indicators of the heat, pressure, etc., shafts and furnaces and many more machines were found there. The long steel shaft leading to the propeller we all duly followed to the end. We were 20 ft below sea level.

On August 1st, about 7 p.m., Coney Island and Long Island came into view. It was not till next day that the tug pulled us to the dock. I took photographs of the Statue of Liberty, the Manhattan skyline, the Brooklyn Bridge and our fellow passengers. We were sorry that our good times were over.

And they sure were. Mum came on board, greeted us icily, said she thought my hair and suit awful and was very nasty indeed. Ulvia and I left her at once.

This was the year of the Dior "New Look", and I had on a lovely dark blue suit with a double cloche skirt and a tight, fitted jacket. My hair was cut short and I thought myself very elegant. I spent a very uncomfortable half hour being told I looked ridiculous in my cherished outfit. I nearly burst into tears. My mother could be perfectly horrid at times, especially if she suspected one of

Ulvia and Ali at the Homestead

us was becoming vain. With her around, there was not much fear of that. There we were in the States with a beastly welcome and feeling miserable and homesick. I've always felt homesick for Egypt, except for the time I left after the revolution.

The press was there on our arrival, to see what little Egyptian princes looked like. So silly!

We had lunch at the St. Regis, where Mum had been staying, but she was not through with us. Criticism, scolding, rude comments, nasty jokes came pouring down on us, especially me. She did not like my hair style, or my suit, or the setting of my ring, in fact nothing. Thankfully, we took the 4.30 train to Washington D.C. and thence to the Mayflower Hotel. At that time, it was the *in* hotel. My mother had a suite and we were given rooms nearby.

Mummy *did* have a nice surprise for us. A few days later, we left for the Homestead, Hot Springs, Virginia. Mummy stayed at the main hotel and we had a chalet in the huge park. It was a beautiful place with tennis, swimming, horseback riding, and lots of young people. Everybody was very well off and very sporty. I went riding and also played bad tennis and tried to swim. I was born with a heart "murmur", which meant that I could not take part in arduous sports. As a child, I'd been carried up the stairs in Garden City and could not swim in the sea but only paddle in shallow water. Now I was allowed to do a bit more, but was very bad at everything, having no practice at all in any sport.

It was about this time that Mr. Frank Rediker made his appearance. He was very nice to us and of course to Mummy.

We got to know lots of boys and girls our age, as well as the dance instructor and his partner. Every few days, there was a dance or a special evening organised for us in the main building. We danced on a terrace giving onto the grounds, which were lit by tiny, coloured lanterns. Very romantic. The dance instructor and his partner were the organisers of most of our evenings and

Nevine at the Homestead

knew how to amuse us. Chaperons were at every corner and apart from a stolen kiss or two, there was no "funny business" going on. The only boy I met again later was Taylor Bigbie, whose family were great friends of Mary Holmes, one of Mum's new bosom pals. He was a nice boy and never tried anything at all, not even a kiss on the cheek. I obviously did not inspire him and all the family relationships were enough to put one off any way.

When the holidays were over, we returned to Washington. Ulvia was enrolled in Madeira School and in September, Mum, Mr. Rediker, Ulvia and I set off to visit the school in Mum's new Cadillac. The school was in the Virginia countryside overlooking the Potomac river. Miss Madeira, aka Mrs. Wing, met us and took us to her study. Then another mistress arrived, obviously the real head of the school, Mrs. Wing, being rather old and slightly tottering in the upper regions, only standing as the figure head. It was all a rather painful business, what with Mrs. Wing comparing us to Japs and Chinese and Mr. Rediker trying his best to keep up a polite conversation. He must have been scared stiff that Mum would let the ladies have a piece of her mind.

Then Ali was enrolled in Staunton Military Academy to his absolute horror and left us on September 14th. It did him a lot of good, as he'd become a spoilt, whiny pest.

I was left by myself with nothing to do. Mummy had a full social life and not one she could drag a teenage daughter to. There was one dinner I was allowed to attend because it was her invitation at the Mayflower. The guests were the *gratin* of Washington, Mr. Royall, Secretary of the Navy with his wife, and General Omar Bradley, no less, with his wife. The ladies, Mrs. Royall and Mrs. Bradley were absolutely charming to a shy, uncomfortable girl and the men all danced with me. Mum's pal, Mrs. Holmes was there, as well as Mr. Rediker. There was a show and I was allowed to drink champagne and after four glasses I was on a rosy cloud.

Bits

I had another outing, this time with Taylor. He invited me to a football game in Charlottesville, Virginia. George Washington vs. Virginia U. GW won 20-12 to our disgust. It was my first and last experience of a weekend at a men's college. A friend of Taylor's, Bart Shore-Kennedy collected me and his date, Elizabeth Hartley, from Charlottesville station, and drove us to the house he and Taylor shared. We drove to the game in separate cars, and after Libbie and I checked our make-up at the house, we all went to a lovely club for dinner, then to Bart's Fraternity. There were lots of drunks and couples dancing in a black, smoky hole, so Taylor and I left and drove to Taylor's house in Lynchburg. His mother was there, but she'd wrenched her back and was in bed. He took me to meet her and she was charming and very pretty.

Next day, he drove me back to the Mayflower and in the evening he took me to friends of his in Alexandria, Virginia. They had a tape recorder, which was a relatively new invention, and we had great fun recording our idiotic conversations. Taylor took me home at 11 p.m. and I was delighted with my day. I was really very modest in my definition of a good time!

I was beginning to worry about Mum's spending. "Where are we going to get the money to live in our grand style in this expensive place?" Looking back, I'm surprised that I realised there would eventually be money problems. My parents rarely mentioned money except in a general way and never frightened us with bankruptcy. I accused her of treating Bits and me like slaves, being inconsiderate and selfish, especially with Bits. I seem to have forgotten that poor Mum was going through a divorce she would never have asked for if Dad had given her some hope.

Bits and I did do some sightseeing. We visited the Washington Monument, the Capitol, the Lincoln Memorial. We also went to the movies when Mum did not require her presence. But Bits had to leave soon and I was going to go mad with nothing to do, knowing nobody my age and having my solitary

Nevine at Bryn Mawr

meals in the Coffee Shop. Mum did take me with her at times, but I did not particularly enjoy these outings, because I was frightfully shy and my small talk was nil. If the people I was speaking to did not contribute most of the conversation, everything ended very quickly and they or I would wander off.

Finally, I told Mum I'd like to go to college, preferably Bryn Mawr. We had paid a visit to the Egyptian Ambassadress, a very polite and pretty lady. Mum got the Ambassador involved. On October 28th, he called Mum to ask her to get in touch with Mrs. Broughton, the Dean of Admissions at Bryn Mawr, who wanted us to come down the next day. I was so excited I could not sleep. Mum told me that Mrs. Broughton had been impressed by my excellent marks and thought it would be good to have me. I would stay for a week and then spend the following weekend in Washington, in case I needed to buy a few things.

* * *

On October 29th, Mum and I boarded the 9 a.m. train to Philadelphia, took the Paoli local to Bryn Mawr station and a cab to Taylor Hall, where Miss McBride, the President of Bryn Mawr College, received us.

We had lunch with the girls and the Warden at Radnor Hall where I would be living. Mum left and the Warden, Miss Utzinger, showed me around the campus.

I met my three compatriots, graduate students who invited me to the Graduate Centre for dinner. They were Wadad Habib, Leila Sharawi and Leila Shoukry. I had a delightful evening and liked them very much. Later in life, I met Wadad and Leila Shoukry again, under different circumstances.

I was studying English, German and French Literature, majoring in French Literature, History and Philosophy. Scholastically, I did quite well, Cum Laude both years and in French got 90s for my essays.

Barry Seymour and Katusha Cheremeteff

Nevine's coming out

I took piano lessons and attended the cultural events in Philadelphia and at College. We heard Eugene Ormandy conduct the Philharmonic and Arthur Rubinstein playing Franck, Chopin, Debussy and Liszt and we saw Margot Fonteyn and Moira Shearer dance.

One weekend in Washington, Mum talked about the situation in Egypt with Bits and me. She thought the British would be back if the King continued in his irresponsible way and would put Prince Abdel Moneim on the throne.

For part of the Christmas vacation, Mummy sent me to the Kramers in New York. Mr. Kramer, once a jeweller in Egypt, had invested money for Mum at a very good rate. He had a beautiful apartment on Fifth Avenue and twin daughters, Mickey and Jackie with whom I got on famously.

It was boring in Washington until Ulvia turned up and we spent the rest of the year together, with occasional visits to Mum. The 31st, we spent drinking cokes and knitting!

My friends at College were Katusha, a Russian countess, Carmen Velasco from Cuba, Iran Ala, daughter of the Iranian Ambassador, Isik Sagmanli from Turkey, and Francine du Plessix from France, New Yorkers Elaine Marks, Barry Seymour, Joanna Semel and Gladys Beck, Betsey Taliaferro from Chevy Chase, Maryland and Sally Watts from St. Louis.

I found out about sex from the College doctor. She showed us how babies were made, mainly to stress the dangers of getting pregnant. If a girl became pregnant, she was removed quietly and quickly from College. I was horrified. My parents did this? The King and Queen? I was scared of and uninterested in sex. Ulvia and Nanou knew all there was to know years before my initiation. When Tata, Nanou's elder sister, had her first period, she told me the most harrowing stories of awful pain and the bed soaked in blood. I did not wish to know the rest. The College doctor's presentation was not very clear – there were still murky areas I carefully avoided. This was not as difficult as one might think. We were supposed to remain virgins until marriage and although some girls did everything BUT, I got nowhere near. I did not go in much for necking and absolutely no petting. Later, Granny asked me what these words meant and I had great difficulty explaining "petting."

We studied a lot, but had quite a good time. One evening, Sally and I went out with a couple of guys for drinks and dancing. In Pennsylvania, you had to be 21 to be served alcohol and we were eighteen. We borrowed a driving license from a Senior as there were no photos on licenses at that time.

We spent the summer of 1949 at the Greenbrier, White Sulphur Springs, West Virginia, another glorious spot. We were disappointed not to return to the Homestead, but Mum decided that a 10% increase was too much. At the Greenbrier, I met Marian and Frederick Bellinger from St. Louis with whom I stayed several times.

Christmas 1949, I was presented to Washington society at a ball at the Mayflower. Mummy had married Frank Rediker to our horror and Daddy's poorly disguised fury. Frank Rediker was a good looking man of fifty who resembled Dad quite a bit. He was very nice to us and we finally accepted him. We did not have much choice. We had no idea that he was an almost professional gigolo who fed on rich women thanks to his looks and good manners. Mum had bought a building on 2339 Mass. Avenue. Our apartment was beautiful, huge with twelve rooms furnished with the best pieces from Garden City, including my Bechstein baby grand.

Back at Bryn Mawr, there was great excitement. Both King Farouk and the Shah of Iran, now divorced, needed heirs. There was a wild rumour around campus that Iran Ala was the future Empress of Iran and I the next Queen of Egypt. The society pages in Washington were full of it. It must have started in Cairo, but when the rumour became international, Daddy and the Palace issued denials. It was rather fun while it lasted. I would have been a disaster as queen, but Iran would have been a perfect empress.

I became a star of the stage instead. Our French teacher, Mr. Guicharnaud, a young, good looking man was putting on Molière's *Monsieur de Pourceaugnac*, a relatively unknown play. I played the female lead and Elaine Marks had the main role. It went well and "even if I was trembling, I acted OK. The audience was wonderful. After numerous curtain calls, Elaine and I shook hands with G (Mr. Guicharnaud), who told me I was a very beautiful Julie." Elaine and I cleaned up, drank wine and showed off.

Nanou sent me a letter telling me that her little nephew Ashraf had died. He had been vaccinated against diphtheria and the serum administered in one dose had been too much for his heart. Years later, I married Ahsraf's father. The death of his son was a terrible experience from which he never recovered. I was to pay part of the price. The rest of the price was to discover at the same time that his wife had been unfaithful for years.

In Washington, I heard that Totes was marrying a Greek girl and Mum was off to Egypt for three weeks. For part of vacation, Ulvia and Ali were invited by school friends and I to Sally Watts' in St. Louis and then to the Bellingers.

I returned to Washington D.C. on June 18. Bits and Ali met me at Union Station. That's when Jack the bellboy and his wife took us to our first baseball game.

Mummy returned from Egypt on June 28th in poor shape. Daddy had behaved very badly. It occurred to me that perhaps it was not all his fault. After the War, she had been very difficult to live with, screaming and scolding everybody, especially poor Dad. She gave no details of the terrible things he had done, but it all had to do with the girlfriend. She said she was through with Egypt and would never go back. Dispirited, almost bitter. I was worried, it was not like her to be beaten so easily.

She was not over Dad. She said how charming but utterly selfish he was,

171

unable to give anything of himself. She said he had wanted her back, but it was too late. She was married to Frank Rediker, who had become a Moslem, so that it was even legal in Egypt. Then she described Dad and her living in Brunoy and how in the evenings he used to do picture puzzles and she would read murder stories out loud.

None of us helped her in what must have been the worst time of her life. It would not have been easy, because the way we had been brought up taught us to suffer alone, preferably in silence.

When Mum saw the state she had put me in, she took me shopping for clothes and bought me a typewriter.

She said Aunt Emina Tugay had asked for my hand in marriage for her nephew, Faizi Muchtar. My answer was no, although he was very rich. Later I found out it was also no on his part because he was in love with an English girl whom he eventually married.

About that time, the King decided to marry a 16-year old girl, named Nariman Sadek, already engaged to a lawyer. This went down badly with everybody, from the Royal Family to the man in the street. The King did his best to lose what remained of his popularity.

Mum phoned to say a girl called Something Zaki was marrying Uncle Saïd Toussoun. I was horrified because of the age difference. I kept hoping it was not true, but a few days later, I received a newspaper cutting from Bits, announcing Nawal Zaki's engagement to Prince Saïd Toussoun.

Taylor was out of favour. I'd invited him to Bryn Mawr for an important weekend and he'd sent a wire at the last minute to say he could not come and letter was following. Weeks later I received the letter, its careless tone was insulting. The sad reason that I'd invited him at all was that he was the only man I knew relatively well.

In March, Mum went to Cairo again. Ali and I met in Washington at the

Mayflower. Mr. Rediker gave us a really good time, meals in the Snake Pit, at the Statler Hotel, the Normandy Inn in Maryland, the Blue Room at the Shoreham, etc.

Mum said we would spend the winter in Cairo. Dad had taken apartments for us in Zamalek. Garden City was sold but not yet empty. At first, we would live there. With hindsight, selling Garden City was a mistake. When the Royal Family was confiscated, only members with titles were confiscated. Mum divorced from Dad had no title and Garden City was in her name, inherited from her father who was not a royal. She could have kept it and sold it for millions.

* * *

I almost missed my train thanks to Sally who had disappeared with my bags. I've nearly missed many a train, but not this barely! Bits met me at Union Station in Washington and took me to 2339 Mass. Avenue, our new home. With Mum and Mr. Rediker (now named Frankenstein), we sat in the bar and chatted till all hours.

One evening after dinner, Mummy began coughing up blood and worried us terribly. At 1 a.m. she was better, but all night I heard Bits and Mr. R. rushing around until the doctor arrived. Next day, she was still sick, but got better later on in the day. We even discussed my taking over the housekeeping in the houses in Egypt. It seems I'd need £E 250 a month for food, wages, gas, petrol and electricity bills.

Next day, Mum was taken to Doctor's Hospital. She was feeling better and looked very pert and cheerful as they took her away in an ambulance. We visited her twice the following day. At midnight we took the train to New York, and from there two taxis to Jersey City, arriving much too early to embark.

The ship finally left, passing Manhattan's wonderful skyline and the Statue of Liberty. I was very sad to leave the States, although not long ago, I was yakking about returning to Egypt.

Our ship was the *Excambion* of the American Export Lines. It was modern if not very big, and the cabins were large and quite comfortable.

It was not only to see us that Dad wanted us to return to Egypt. Complications had began concerning our prolonged stay in America. The King was having a bad time with his mother, who had gone to California with her two younger daughters and refused to come home. She was rumoured to have married and become Catholic. And although Faika did return home married to a Moslem Egyptian, the youngest Fathia married a Copt. The King told Daddy that if Ulvia and I did not return to Egypt, he would remove our titles as he did not want any more members of the Family marrying foreigners and non-Moslems. Daddy did not take kindly to Mr. Rediker, and wanted us to come home anyway. Mummy did not object, except for Ali, who was doing well at Staunton and had stopped being a spoilt brat. Ulvia and I were delighted because, apart from our summer vacations, we were bored to tears in Washington. I was extremely sorry to leave Bryn Mawr. I hoped to return, but it seemed improbable.

Mummy left Egypt with most of our valuables. Neither she nor Daddy seemed to act as though Egypt was about to explode. Daddy had made a million pounds in an arms deal and was spending money furiously on the house in Schutz, cars, girlfriend, and us when we arrived. Mummy was doing the same in Washington. Before the revolution, she received the revenue from her land by cheque or cash. Daddy bought emeralds and diamonds with her Garden City money. She was to sell them as required. He also sent her paintings. When she tried to sell them, she had a terrible time proving they were authentic.

On the *Excambion*, after a first and very negative glance at the other passengers, we soon found a few kindred spirits. There was a good-looking Catholic priest we all fell in love with, a red Englishman of dubious attractiveness, and an Egyptian called Sammy Michael who came up to meet the "princesses." Then there were the two lovely daughters of the Delacortes of publishing fame, Marianna and Margarita, and Mickey, the lovely daughter of the equally prestigious Gehan family.

We were soon busy with all kinds of activities: ping pong, the slot machines, Black Jack, Bingo, and dancing. Father McCallen joined in all the games. We often went to bed at 3 a.m. I for one slept late in the morning. There were movies every day and some people gave cocktail parties. Mickey Gehan for one, and then Sami. There were truly few boring moments.

Arriving at Marseilles, we three and Bits took a cab to the Hotel Splendide and from there drove to Notre Dame de la Garde, a beautifully decorated church. Next morning, we went off to Arles and Avignon. We stopped at Martigues, an exquisite little fishing village on the Lac de Berre, a painter's dream. In Arles, we visited the Roman arena and amphitheatre and the cloisters of an old church, where we met up with Mr. Gehan, Captain Kuhne and Father. We dined at a charming little hotel and went on to Avignon, where we inspected the Pope's Palace, a huge, white stone pile. The rooms were enormously high and large and some were hung with the most gorgeous Gobelin tapestries. We returned to the ship via Aix-en-Provence and later that night we sailed for Naples.

Next evening, we had the Captain's formal dinner and got all dressed up. We drank champagne, danced, sang and drank more champagne. We ended in the Purser's office, having a great old time. Margarita thanks to the champagne offered to kiss Father. He told me afterwards that he was tempted. He and I shook hands "warmly."

We arrived in Naples very early in the morning. Adèle, Bits' lovely ex sister-in-law, came to take us to Capri, but Ulvia and Ali were feeling rather sick, so I ended by going off with her by myself. We boarded a boat to Capri with her sister, Olga, and an Italian man. We first went to the Hotel Cesare Augustus, situated on the top of a cliff with a magnificent view. We had drinks and then walked to see the Faraglioni, strangely formed rock piles jutting out of the water; lunched at a seaside restaurant and took a motorboat to the Blue Grotto. To my surprise, the grotto was really blue, a perfectly beautiful blue. The water is bright blue, the walls of the cave reflecting it.

The following days were a let-down. The voyage was nearly over and we were sad to have lost some of our new friends and were on the eve of losing the others. What awaited us? There was great happiness to see Dad and a life without Mum breathing heavily down our necks.

We finally arrived in Alexandria on June 29th. Bits woke us at 8 a.m. and we docked at 10 o'clock. Dad was there with Mahgoub Effendi and Farrag Effendi and we got the full treatment: first to leave the ship, police escort, etc.

It is difficult to remember that marvellous time when one did not have to queue up, be insulted by all and sundry for no reason, become exhausted with delays and general mismanagement of which all authorities are so proud. I don't feel the least guilty and only regret those great times. I don't care if other people have to go through trying experiences, as I'm sure they could not care what happens to me. That does not mean I'm not willing to help people, but I refuse to help those who are too lazy to bother. I'm against lowering standards because some people can't attain them. Today, even entrance exams in some universities must be as easy as possible to ensure a majority of students qualify. Why? Some don't want to go to university, but are pushed by their parents, teachers, friends. There is nothing wrong in being a good carpenter, gardener or cook, and a good deal safer for the rest of us than being a bad doctor.

Ulvia with Marianna and Margarita Delacorte on the Excambion

***

I can pass to you
Generations of roses in this wrinkled berry
There; now you hold in your hand a race
Of summer gardens, it lies under centuries of petals.

Christopher Fry, *The Lady's not for burning*

***

We reached Schutz at 11 a.m. The garden was beautiful, but Dad had transformed the house into a "hunting lodge." The walls in the hall, salons and dining room were now panelled in dark brown. Most of the furniture was from Garden City, the huge bookcases, the refectory table and chairs from the dining room, and the brown leather and velvet cushioned sofa and chairs from the small salon. When Mummy bought Schutz, she had furnished it with Grandpa's very modern furniture from Helwan. In my opinion, the house then was more agreeable and certainly sunnier. Dad had also built a huge fireplace in one of the living rooms in place of a window, which made the room very dark. I must admit the fireplace was a godsend, Alexandria winters are very cold and there is no central heating. He had also installed beautiful parquet in the reception area and the windowpanes were coloured glass, which with the panelling must have cost a fortune. Spending all this money when he was supposedly convinced the country was about to explode seems quite mad. Mummy was doing much the same in Washington D.C.

We went to see Granny who was very nice to us. I don't know why it

Princess Kerima Halim

The Halim sisters: from left (seated) Princesses Wijdan, Kerima, Emina and Tewfika; (standing) Nimet, and Zenab Abbas Halim

seemed to have surprised us. We also called Mum on the phone at 7 p.m.

Next day I was 20! We went to town to get dresses and bathing suits. Granny came to lunch with Ulla, her lady companion. We all had a siesta, and at 5 p.m. Aunts Kerima and Emina Halim, Dad's first cousins, arrived. They were among the most beautiful women in Egypt. Egypt had many beautiful women, mostly members of the Royal Family.

Dad took me to the garage to show me the Cadillac convertible he was giving me as a birthday present. I nearly died with joy. Mum informed me later that it was *her* car and *her* present. After Granny and the aunts left, Sambo and I took the car out and I drove it home on Abukir Road.

Next day we went to see our Izzet cousins. Bahia was very slim, with short hair, dyed a reddish colour I disliked. I was very jealous of her slimness and immediately decided to go on a diet. Aleya, her younger sister, and Leila, a cousin to all of us, had not changed. We all laughed hysterically in the garden. We dined there, joined by Leila's parents, Uncle Mohamed, Mum's first cousin, his wife, Aunt Sherifa and Aunt Aicha, his sister. To clear up this cousin business again, cousins can mean anything from second to fourth cousins, if they are our generation. Cousins of our parents were invariably called Aunt and Uncle.

Dad showed us around the Royal Automobile Club of which he was president. He had chosen the spot high up on rocks giving onto the sea. The building was unpretentious like a chalet. Outside, bars, tables and chairs under umbrellas surrounded the pool, inside there was a restaurant and gambling rooms. Daddy was justifiably proud of both this club and the Cairo one. They were very well run, with an excellent staff of waiters, cooks, barmen and women attendants. In summer, the top staff would move to Alexandria. Members of the staff were proud to be chosen and Dad had a difficult time deciding who would go to Alex. There was no problem about the Head Waiter,

Head Cook and Head Barman, but the lesser lights were a headache. One great idea was bringing François, the hairdresser, to work in the very pretty little *Salon de Coiffure*. The ladies were delighted.

Dad took us to lunch at the Yacht Club where tables were set out on flower-draped terraces descending to the harbour. There we met Countess Yolande de Zogheb, the mysterious girl friend, who was really very nice. She must have been terrified of us, knowing our reputation.

On to Cairo. Dad woke us up at 6 a.m. and we were on our way at 7 in three cars. Dad and Ulvia picked up the Countess. We reached Garden City around 10 o'clock. The Countess did not live there, she had her own flat near the Automobile Club.

Garden City looked much the same if rather empty in some places. It was still home and we only wished Mum could have been with us.

We visited our grandfather, Prince Ibrahim. He looked very pale and weak, but was as full of life as his health would allow. He seemed to be a great person and certainly charmed me. We never knew why he and Dad were estranged. He had been blind for a long time and carried this terrible affliction with courage and grace.

We lunched at the Lenoses with Toppy our Turkish housekeeper and sometime chaperon and my friend from the English School, Helen Constantinidis. Totes came to see us at home in the afternoon. My comments on his person are best forgotten.

We were back in Alex on July 5th, and having received a call from Marianna Delacorte, we agreed to have lunch on the *Excambion* the next day. We were greeted with great joy and enthusiasm by all our friends and when the ship finally sailed, most of the passengers were on deck waving goodbye to us.

We met Dad and the Countess at Pastroudis, Dad's favourite bar and restaurant in Alexandria, the owner and his wife being special friends of his.

Nevine in Caddy

Wherever we went, we were always beautifully treated thanks to Dad and not only because of the title.

There was *the* dressmaker, Madame Solange who bought originals from the best houses in Paris and copied them for her clients. She had very good taste, and was a prominent figure in society married to Mandara Ralli, of a well-known Greek family.

Dad took us to dinner at Aunt Emina Halim's and her husband Sabry Bey Bayindir. Princess Marie-Louise of Bulgaria, the daughter of King Boris, was there and after an enormous dinner, we sat around talking about the cynicism of creation. Later Dad and Sabry Bey did card tricks to our delight. We'd had enough of the intellectual stuff.

We were calling Mum and/or Mr. Rediker frequently. She was still in hospital after an operation for a tumour on the lung, which thank God was benign. It was her old story with her teeth poisoning her system.

With our own cabin not far from Uncle's, we spent a lot of time walking back and forth to see our cousins, generally meeting mid-way. This was when Rose el Youssef, a magazine with a society page, published a pen drawing of me with the caption "Nevine Halim with bucket and broom." At times, I swept the sand out of the cabin and a roving reporter must have seen me at work. I was furious. The drawing was most unflattering, but my friends found it extremely funny. A delightful lot!

My driving had reached the dangerous stage and I scraped the mudguard off a small car. Sambo would not let me go off by myself, but at one point I had to drive alone or I'd never learn. One morning, I had a fitting at Madame Solange's and could not find Sambo, so I drove my car to town. I even managed to park without a major disaster. Of course, there were fewer cars and wonderful people called *munadis* who would park your car for a small tip. Sambo was livid. He was not only afraid I'd smash myself up but furious that

I'd disobeyed him. I was really quite frightened by his reaction. Dad said Sambo was right and I should not have gone off without a word to anybody. Still, that's how I learned to drive.

Having ordered clothes from Mme Solange, we now had to buy shoes. With Mme de Z, we went to the famous shoemaker, Artur. He made exquisite shoes and could copy any model you wanted. He was terribly expensive: £E 10 a pair. An enormous sum those days. We now had evening and cocktail dresses, but needed morning frocks and pants. Mme de Z took us shopping for the missing items. She was a good soul, so helpful and polite, a great sense of humour, and she adored Dad. She was born a Zogheb and her mother was responsible for turning her into a "courtesan." It was rumoured that she had started her career with the King, but it did not last long. For her good luck she fell on Dad, who treated her with the utmost respect and kindness. When it was over, he organised her marriage to a very rich man called Bouez. We even went to their beautiful apartment in Guezira for a celebratory drink.

I've barely mentioned Victor Bersolesi, a former heavy-weight boxer, called Battling Vic, befriended by Daddy and now his days of glory over, he worked as a supervisor of the garden, the various live-stock, etc. We treated poor Berso very badly, but he took it all quite well. Sometimes when we really overdid things, he'd refuse to speak to us and threaten to tell Dad, but he never did.

A business acquaintance of Dad's, Mahmoud Fahmy, had given me a gorgeous baby chow. He was so cuddly and his fur so silky, we could not stop playing with him. His name was Mish Mish, which means apricot in Arabic, but I changed it to Toffee as his fur was just that colour.

Ulvia and I chose this time to go on a diet. It lasted only a few days, because besides feeling deathly ill, we became so weak we could scarcely move. After a good meal, we felt human again.

Our "sweet coz" Bahia was in love again to our despair. Ulvia and I could not understand why she and her sister refused to meet the objects of their infatuation. It's not much good, mooning over somebody from afar. And these "objects" were mostly perfectly respectable boys. Of course, this did not include her violent passion for famous sportsmen. I must say there were a few gorgeous specimen, highly unsuitable for Bahia. Uncle would have had a fit if he'd found out. She wanted to get married as soon as possible because she was not getting on with her stepmother, Auntie Maria. She refused most eligible proposals, accepting one about a year later, from Zaki Serageldine, the younger brother of Fouad Pasha Serageldine, Minister of Interior in the Wafd government. They had nothing in common and after producing two sons, she divorced him. To her eternal credit, she brought up her sons herself with little help from Zaki, who remarried and had other children. Her sons, Abdallah and Fouad are worthy of her. She sent them to school in Switzerland, where they remained after the revolution. They married Swiss girls, became Swiss and have good jobs. Abdallah has four sons and Fouad one lovely daughter. To my great sorrow, Bahia left us recently. There are no more calls asking why I've taken so long to phone her, no more discussions about anything that might come to her bright mind, no more laughs that only we could share. Granny told me that to live too long is dreadful, although she had her son and grandchildren, there was nobody left with whom to talk about people and events of her youth, nobody who could understand those days, now gone forever, a second time.

At the Automobile Club, we met just about *everybody*. I'll spare you a long list of people, some well-known, some not. It did not seem to matter much. We avoided the stuffy ones and became friends with the others. The sons of Laky and Alice Zervudachi, great friends of our parents, introduced us to the young set. Nolly the older son, we'd not met before, but Marke had been at the English School at the same time as us. Thanks to them we were soon part of the social whirl, a pretty royal whirl too. During the war, many of the royal families of Europe had been made welcome in Egypt by King Farouk: the King and Queen of Italy, with their daughters and grandchildren; the King and Queen of Albania; the King of Bulgaria and his mother; the King, Crown Prince and Crown Princess of Greece; the King of Yugoslavia; Prince and Princess Roman Romanoff and their sons, Nicholas and Dimitri; Prince Moritz of Hesse. The young members of these families were only too glad to participate in all available amusements. They were innocent amusements: beach parties, balls, dances at various hotels and private houses, invitations aboard visiting ships. And we had fun. Of course, there were love affairs, but mostly platonic. Remember there was no *pill* then, and none of us girls, and boys for that matter, wanted to get into trouble.

The mentality of all classes was very different from now. There was little of the envy which seems so prevalent today, be you rich or poor. Young girls as well as matrons did their best to look attractive. I've watched fashion shows on TV in stunned amazement. The famed generation gap with my parents has nothing to do with the abyss between me and the young of today. I cannot imagine why everybody has to look a mess, some downright dirty.

Among our more intimate friends were Zoë Rees and Jocelyn Draycott, English girls and the de Jenners, Swiss girls. We loved Bernard de Zogheb who wrote the society page in *La Réforme Illustrée,* the French language Alexandria paper. He described the function we attended and what we wore. I had a favourite dress, dark blue with silvery stars and poor Bernie wrote it up in every way he could until one day he begged me to wear something else. Bernie was frightfully funny, singing arias from famous operas in Arabic with Johnny Nahman or with a frightful accent in English. The themes were appalling and unrepeatable. We saw a lot of Robert and Ludovica Gasche, the granddaughter of the King of Italy, and Edouard and Irene Catseflis, he a Greek lawyer and she a melancholy Pole, among the first to have a *chalet* in Agami. There was no electricity in Agami and only a trickle of dirty water, but it was fun if rudimentary.

Dad had a small yacht, the *Nimr*, which he owned with Victor Simeika. We boarded at the Yacht Club and sailed to Nelson Island, opposite Abukir. There we met up with Mahmoud Fahmy, his brother, and Mohamed Hamada on their boat. They accepted an invitation from Dad to come over for a drink and as Mohamed was boarding the dinghy, he fell into the sea. We were hysterical with laughter because he was beautifully dressed in a white shirt, white sharkskin trousers and white shoes. But he was a good sport and climbed on board soaking wet. Dad gave him a *bournous* while a sailor went to fetch dry clothes from the other boat. Our manners were appalling and we teased him mercilessly until Dad told us to shut up. The Dragoshes, she was Loutfia Fadel, great friends of both Dad and Yolande, were with us and thankfully laughed as much as we did. Next day, Ismaïl Muchtar, a cousin of Dad's, arrived in his motor boat and insisted on taking some of us fishing. The victims were Yolande and me and we spent three ghastly hours in the hot sun, almost succumbing to heat stroke and not catching a single fish.

At a party given by the Laky Zervudachis in their beautiful apartment on Avenue de Belgique, we met Princess Faiza and her husband, Bulent. At one point, dancing with Nolly, I executed my newest trick and threw him over my shoulder. Then I tried to trip up Dimitri Romanoff but missed and he landed on top of me on the floor. The Princess was delighted with these rather outlandish amusements, because she was so tired of boring and stuffy parties. Princess Faiza was the King's second sister. She had charm, was generous and kind, and incredibly beautiful. I have never seen her look anything but lovely, not at the beach, in the early hours of the morning, or anytime at all. Bulent was a great organiser and he soon adopted Ulvia and me and included us in all his projects. He was aided by Adel Sabit, who became chief camera operator

Prince Abbas Halim aboard the Nimr in Abukir Bay

when we started making films. Adel was one of Totes' best friends and was related to Queen Nazli through his mother. He worked for the Arab League as assistant to Abdel Rahman Azzam Pasha. Like Bulent, he was full of ideas and also had the willingness and ingenuity to carry them out. Thanks to them, we never had a dull moment.

I would like to introduce members of the *Zohria Group*, so-called because Princess Faiza's house in Cairo was situated in Zohria Gardens, which gave on the golf course of the Guezira Sporting Club. First, some clarification on *groups*. Ulvia and I soon found we belonged to several different groups: the Sidi Bishr group of cousins and old friends, the Royal Automobile Club group, mostly Daddy's friends, and finally, but far from last, the Zohria Group. Ulvia and I did not always travel together. Of course, we generally attended the same big events, but we had different "special" friends and in our everyday activities we tended to go our separate ways. Not at all surprising as you could not find two more dissimilar people. We got on well enough as long as we had a breather from each.

The leaders of the Zohria Group, of course, were Faiza and Bulent; but she let him lead and followed, laughing ruefully at times as when he took all her marvellous materials destined to re-cover the living room and bedroom furniture to make a tent for one of his films. She refused to appear in any of our epics, and how right she was. The films were perfectly innocent, indeed often quite idiotic, but they were all confiscated at the time of the revolution, and heaven knows what somebody with evil intent could fabricate about them and about her. Gossip began way before the revolution. Mostly we laughed at it, but sometimes it was truly disgusting. The dirt was frequently invented by people, not in our group, who were jealous and vented their rage by telling revolting stories about our activities. They would have been extremely disappointed: sitting on the carpet playing tiddly-winks, squealing with joy

Princess Faiza

when we managed to "tiddle" a "wink." The dreadful "orgies" would have disappointed them even more. Apart from formal parties, when we were all in evening dress, "all tarted up" to put it vulgarly, we wore nothing very fancy. Of course, Princess Faiza had to be perfect at all times, and she was. So we watched movies, filmed *our* movies, talked politics, had horrendous discussions on every possible subject, listened to music, etc.

The house itself was no palace. It was comfortably large. As you walked in, barely escaping being bitten by Tse, Faiza's chow, you found yourself in a large hall. The drawing room, a small library giving onto it, was on the right, the bar in front of you and the dining room, only used for official dinners, far to the left. We spent most of our time, depending on the weather, either on the terrace in front of the bar, in the bar itself or in the drawing room. The house was beautifully furnished by Bulent, who was also warmly welcoming. There were three floors, the last one comprising a modern kitchen and a movie theatre. There was no swimming pool, but there were two tennis courts. The garden gave onto the Guezira Sporting Club and thus had the benefit of an extended stretch of green comprising the golf course and race track. We could easily walk from Faiza's house to the Club, which we sometimes did if we left a car here or there. Very important: Faiza's servants were very well-trained, with beautiful manners. Her *maître d'hotel* was a very important man in the Sudan, obliged to make a living in Egypt as his country had no decent jobs to offer. He was a proud man, always treated with the utmost courtesy by his master and mistress and completely devoted to them.

To describe our hostess and host in more detail is extremely difficult, especially Faiza. She always behaved perfectly, rarely got annoyed or showed that she was bored. And she had to put up with horrendous bores, people who would corner her until one of us went to save her. Bulent could be impossible at times, but she had a great deal of patience with him. He was a

192

very cultured man, a cousin to all of us, as his grandmother was Princess Fatma, a daughter of Khedive Ismaïl. Princess Fatma sold all her magnificent jewels to build the first university in Cairo. She also donated the land on which it was built. On his father's side he was Turkish. Faiza and Bulent's marriage lasted as long as they were in Egypt. Once in Europe, the difficulties began, mostly financial. Faiza did manage to get out most of her jewels, but she had no talent for money management. She was quite capable of going into a shop and buying twenty twin sets, ten bags and twenty pairs of shoes. Even when she was in Egypt, she was always in debt. And Bulent was just as bad. She joined her mother in Los Angeles after the divorce and he worked in London, went to Turkey, set himself up as a kind of guru, and even married again. We only met once again, in a night club in Geneva.

Let us return to Zohria and the people most actively involved in our doings: Adel Sabit, his cousins, Saleh and Fayed Sabit, our cousin Prince Hassan Hassan, his elder brother Ismaïl, Pier Francesco Calvi di Bergolo, commonly called Piffo, and in spite of that grandson to the King of Italy, Prince Namouk of Turkey, Prince Fouad of Turkey, called "Uncle Ossi" by intimates, although he was pretender to the Imperial Ottoman throne. We also had Bob Simpson, Private Secretary to the American Ambassador, supposedly a great friend.

There were members not always available, either because of work, travel, or because they lived in Alexandria. The Alexandrians were the Stagni brothers, Carlo, Sandro and Ernesto, whose father made a fortune in wood; Donatella and Lanfranco Spechel, whose father was the Italian Consul in Alexandria; Samiha Khayat from a great Coptic family; the Zervudachi clan now included Giovanna and Virginia, cousins of Nolly and Marke. The Zervudachis' great-grandfather Draneht Pasha worked for Khedive Ismaïl and was well rewarded, mostly with land. Then came the Romanoff boys. Moritz of Hesse, another grandson of the King of Italy, whose mother Princess Mafalda had died in a

Prince Dimitri Romanoff

Nazi concentration camp. Petti (Pierre) Bless, a Swiss whose family among other things owned a large piece of Agami, a resort outside Alex. The British contingent were represented by Lord Westbury, Eddie Gathorne-Hardy, Felicity Ingleby-Machenzie, and James Murray, First Secretary at the British Embassy. Lastly there was Stefan Boideff, a mad Bulgarian and former ADC to his King. Stalwarts were also Samira and Samiha Wahba, from another well-known Coptic family; Annamaria and Max Edrei, a sought-after architect, scion of a rich Jewish family. The Camaras were Greek, Marquis Luis de Perinat was First Secretary at the Spanish Embassy and his colleague was Gabriel Martinez de Matta. Not to be forgotten was Jojo Nahoum, son of the Grand Rabbi of Egypt, a wonderful pianist whether in classical or jazz music and a man of enormous culture who never showed off. The South American diplomats were prime favourites. Jorge Sorrondo, who later married the Polish countess Sybilla Szczeniowska, a good portrait painter; his great pal Carlito Stegmann played the guitar wondrously; and the Argentine Minister, Willy Speroni. Some of these diplomats were also world-champion polo players, like Pancho Bengoleya, so handsome. Egypt had a very good polo team, consisting of Wahid Pasha Yousry and officers of the Royal Cavalry.

Most of these people were regularly summoned to Zohria by Bulent in order to carry out his latest project. It could be a film, an excursion, a trip to Upper Egypt, a special fancy dress party, a visit to a newly-discovered and interesting archaeological find. They were not a group of party-going nincompoops. In fact, they all brought considerable baggage, besides an ability to hold their liquor and go without sleep. Hassan Hassan was not only an accomplished pianist, but also a painter; Niny Camara was a world champion bridge player; Luis de Perinat became Ambassador to the Court of St. James and later to France; Sir James Murray was British Ambassador to the United Nations in Geneva. Of course, not all of us had brilliant careers, but none was a nonentity.

Our best party in Alexandria that summer was the marriage of Dad's cousin, Ibrahim Fazil to Marcelle Ades. The bride was so happy and proud to be marrying into the Royal Family that the wedding cake she'd ordered was smothered in crowns. Not all were the same, some were imperial crowns to our undisguised glee. The guests were older people and our crowd. After the happy couple left, Dad who'd been strong armed into having the wedding in his house, decided that a little hell-raising was in order. He told the band to play Chopin's funeral march while we solemnly threw the rest of the wedding cake out of the window.

Next day, we lunched at the Zervudachi's farm, *Diffichou*, where Dad described the wedding to those who had not attended. The bride, no spring chick, had asked Yolande if she should wear white and a veil. Yolande in a failing voice suggested she choose another colour and definitely no veil. To our intense relief, Marcelle appeared in a long pale blue organdy gown with a large pale blue organdy hat.

That summer I fell "in love" and after a good deal of manoeuvring and lots of patience, I finally landed the "object of my affection", Prince Dimitri Romanoff. He had initially fallen for Ulvia, but she had a vast court of admirers and was not about to limit herself to one person, so that I was able to console him and it worked! He was and is a darling. We got on very well and only broke up when Cairo people like myself moved back in winter. Dimitri lived and worked in Alexandria, so apart from occasional weekends, we scarcely saw each other. And we all know how separation works. But we had that summer. I'm glad to say that we all made the most of it. Dad had somehow found out about Dimitri and was extremely worried. He asked Yolande and Ulvia if I cared for Dimitri and both said no. This was nonsense, but we never considered our involvement as serious.

Our days and nights were certainly full: the beach, the Automobile Club, the Yacht Club, Agami, Abukir, all the various lunches, teas, parties and balls, the Romance for dinner and dancing. There was nearly always something or somebody new to amuse us. There were drinks at Baudrot's, the *in* tea-room, with Charlie de Zogheb, Costia Mitarachi, Zoë Rees, etc. Our favourite night spot was the Cabana, which had just opened.

An example of a particularly full day was a lunch at Petti Bless in Agami, after which he played the accordion for two solid hours while we sang along rather raggedly. At 5 p.m., we went in for a swim. Faiza, Bulent and Fayed had arrived at 2 and left at 7 p.m. Adel picked up Dimitri and me at 8.30 to go the Catseflis'. Next day at noon, we visited Granny where "we all got hell." From there I went to the hairdresser's, arriving home at 2 p.m. A rest and at 5, Ulvia and I went to the Athineos' for tea. Found Nicholas, Jean-Louis and Johnny Christou there. We all went home to change and at 8, Johnny picked us up to go to Faiza's for dinner. The usual crowd was there on the beautiful roof garden. We all drank vodka. Dimitri had ten and nearly fell asleep. How he didn't pass out, must be due to his Russian blood. He even managed to dance "Golden Earrings" with me, our song. Ulvia and I left at 3.15 a.m.

One last party to remember that summer was to celebrate Daddy's birthday on October 9th. It started very badly as all the lights went out at 7.30 and we had to dress and make-up in candle light. Some of the guests arrived before the lights came on, thankfully just before the arrival of Princess Faiza, beautiful in white. All the dresses were lovely that evening, everybody drank a lot and danced madly until 5.30 a.m. This did not prevent me from having tea with Jocelyn at Baudrot's the following day, rushing home to change to go to Faiza's at 8 to view our first film. It was great, although the story was obscure and the lighting equally so. To my amazement, I was pretty good, except for one place where I laughed.

This went on all summer. Probably the most beautiful summer of our lives.

We were young, healthy, carefree, not very rich, and sometimes quite poor. Our amusements did not cost much and if they did, there was always one member of the gang, or a parent, who had the means to help out, or had had a windfall. We generally preferred not to ask our parents for money beyond our allowances. I remember going to the movies only after pooling our resources. Afterwards, we'd go to our favourite juice and ice-cream stand for a delicious *kaymak* (mastique) ice. If we were hungry there was a *fool* shop next door, small round pita breads filled with horse beans, *fool* in Arabic, the staple food of Egyptians, both filling and energising. These amusements were shared mostly with our Sidi Bishr set and included distant cousins: Djehanquir, Bourhan and Shehriar Rateb (Ulvia married Shehriar), the Abousbahs, the Sabrys and the Yeghens.

Our other set at the Auto Club with Daddy was older and richer—we paid nothing and put everything on Dad's bill. We were often invited by his pals and taken out to night-clubs and bars by the more trustworthy ones. Mohamed Hamada, who'd been married to our Aunt Malek, was a great favourite. Jackie Djeddah was our *souffre-douleur*; if we needed an escort, poor Jackie was shanghaied and forced to take us. One famous night in Cairo, Ulvia and I, in our respective cars, had taken Jackie and Mohamed Hamada to the Auberge des Pyramides, the *in* place. On the way home, Ulvia, at times a reckless driver, smashed into a donkey-cart full of water melons. Mohamed and I were in the car behind and he was driving. Jackie immediately disappeared because there was a great deal of anti-Jewish feeling then and he did not want to face a police inquiry. Mohamed fixed everything by paying the poor man for his water melons and telling Ulvia, whose car had been dented but still ran, to drive to our garage and hide the car. Daddy had just come home and was suspicious when he saw us with Mohamed and the door of Ulvia's garage pulled down. He pulled up the door and she had to come clean. For once, Daddy really scolded her. She was his favourite child, Ali was Mum's and I was Granny's. They pretended they loved us equally, but we knew better. Children are instinctive little brutes and hard to fool in such matters.

* * *

We were back in Cairo still living in Garden City. We arrived in a 4-car convoy on November 5th, a Sunday. I was tired but could not sleep, so I unpacked and at 8.30, Ulvia and I joined Dad and Yolande at the Automobile Club. *The Patron*, i.e. His Majesty was there. I found him not nearly as fat or unattractive as expected. He stared at Ulvia and me until he went into the gambling rooms. I thought he had some appeal, not only based on his rank. Later he asked Dad how come Ulvia and I were allowed into the Club. Dad told him that members of the Royal Family are automatically members in all the clubs in Egypt.

Our activities soon geared up to the Alex level. Faiza and Bulent were in residence at Zohria, we had the Sporting and Auto clubs as other venues, and life was soon as hectic as ever. I met Maria Pilar, a friend of Nanou's from Paris. She was a very ugly girl with terrific vim. She had been a flirt of Dimitri's it seems, but it was very hard to imagine them together. She was a great addition to our group.

Bulent was soon ready to organise our activities, now centred on movie-making. First we viewed the final cut of our first film. It had taken place in Agami, and in spite of heroic efforts to clarify it, the story line was confusing. It was a weird love story. I was the heroine and Johnny Christou, whose family owned all the cinemas in Alex, was the hero. Lots of ghastly things happened to us until the final scene, where I walk into the sea, presumably to commit suicide. Instead of being dramatic, it was hilariously funny. Bulent got the hint

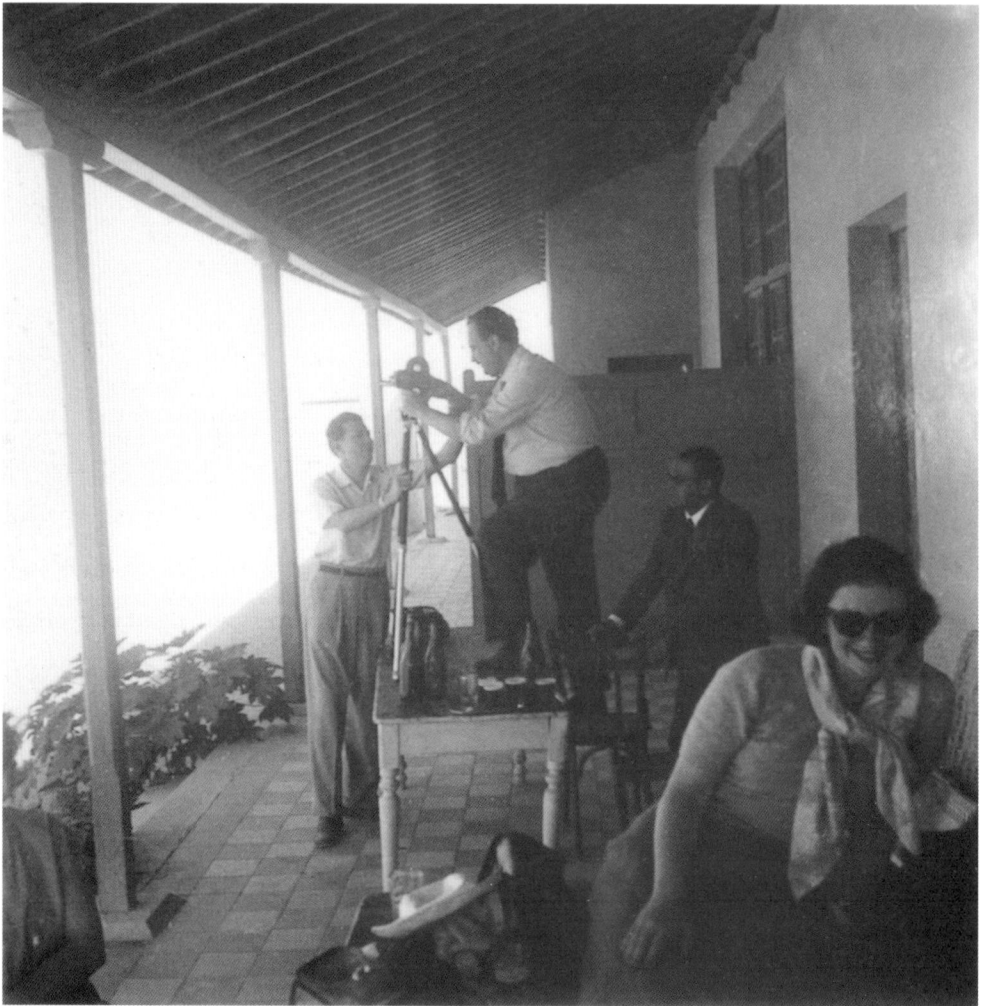

Making movies

and our next subject was Aida, with men portraying women, and vice versa. Prince Namouk of Turkey, very tall and fat, was Amneris, Donatella Spechel, tall and slim was Radames, Johnny Christou was Aida and I was Pharaoh, short and plump. Hassan Hassan and Irene Catseflis were courtesans.

Bulent gathered us under the Sphinx's nose to shoot a very important scene. Lighting was with magnesium flares. Adel, with a new camera, was trying out every angle, while tourists watched obviously thinking this was the real thing. I, as Pharaoh, was seated on a bench just below the Sphinx's head. Aida and Radames cavorted in front of me, a very strange couple. Bulent soon got sick of the real Aida story, even with the sex switches, and allowed himself some peculiar additions. We had a lot of trouble keeping a straight face, as rude suggestions were yelled at us by the stage managers and various hangers-on.

Bulent decided to end Aida and begin a real movie. The new camera was to film this epic. I was the heroine again and Salah Orabi, my husband to be but we did not know it then, was the hero. This new attempt was filmed near Sakkara in the desert. In one scene, Salah had to save me from Bobby Saab, by picking me up onto his saddle and riding off into the sunset. Bobby was on a camel and kept falling off, to our undisguised delight. Poor boy, he was very brave and kept getting back onto the camel. Salah refused point blank to pick me up, and galloped off into the sunset all by himself. Bulent thought this was great and asked him to do it again. Salah told him in no uncertain terms that he refused utterly and completely to ever get on a horse again. He'd never been on a horse before and when the horrible animal took off, he'd just held on, praying for a miracle. So the end of the story was rather odd. Even odder were some of the scenes. Perhaps to compensate Namouk for his boring Amneris role, Bulent now had him playing an Oriental potentate lying in a tent, made up with Faiza's beautiful materials, surrounded by some of the loveliest girls in Cairo society dressed in not much. This had nothing to do with the story of the film, but that did not bother Bulent in the least. It could be used in another movie.

We had a few more birthday parties; Ulvia's on November 7 on the Semiramis roof, and next day Faiza's birthday at Zohria. The 9th was Granny's birthday, we went with Dad to Maadi to pay her a visit.

That evening, I went to the Auto and sat at the bar with Yolande. HM was there and kept looking at us. Mohamed Hamada joined us for dinner and received four messages from HM asking him to play poker with him. One time in Alex, HM commandeered Daddy into gambling with him as the usual players had not turned up. Daddy was furious, but could not refuse. As soon as the King's crowd arrived, Dad immediately left the table, livid with rage. I could not understand why. Generally, Dad did not lose his temper. Ulvia told me that when she got home that evening, the phone was ringing. It was Queen Nariman asking to speak to Dad and when Ulvia told her he had not yet arrived, she gave Ulvia a message for Dad, apologising for her husband's bad manners. Quite a surprise!

I chose to become serious about my education. I arranged with Professor Carro to have piano lessons and pestered Dad to get me into the American University via the American Ambassador. I was going to practice piano four hours a day and spend the rest of my time studying. In the meantime, I went to the Auto Club for lunch, joining the Governor of Cairo, Ghazali Bey, his step-daughter Zisette, and Zoë. At 3, Zoë and I went to the Sporting to play tennis for two hours. Then I had tea at Lilian Besso's, now Mrs. Raiss, and met up with Maryse Amiel and Diana Dwek, also from the English School. I was home at 7, and at 9.30 went to the Auto. HM was there and I had to walk past him to get to the bar. The unofficial protocol was that he was incognito and you pretended not to see him. He kept looking at us at the bar. Rather unnerving, but he soon went off to gamble to our relief.

*Harry Cushing, Nevine, Adel Sabet, Letha Little, Luis de Perinat
and Samiha Wahba at the Semiramis Grill*

Ulvia and Princess Faiza

We had a lovely weekend with the Alex crowd arriving "au complet." We went to a party at the new Princess Marcelle Fazil's house and ended at the opening night of the Scarabée. We found His Majesty there, but he did not stay long. The Scarabée and the Auberge des Pyramides were among his favourite spots, apart from the Auto Club of course. He possessed very high-powered cars and would drive through town at a horrific speed, followed by his bodyguards. Thank God, he was a very good driver. The minute he appeared on the horizon, everybody immediately removed themselves from his trajectory.

Nanou, now Princess Toussoun, was back from Paris. Ulvia and I went to see her and found she had not changed at all. She was pregnant and very plump for the first time in her life. Maria Pilar was there too. After that, we went to the Stevenson's cocktail party, which I found a dreadful bore. From there to the Auto, where the Assems joined us, and then the Auberge to end at the Scarabée. Bed at 4 a.m. The Stevensons must have been the British Ambassador, Sir Ralph Stevenson, but I cannot remember ever having set foot in the British Embassy.

This outline of my activities is mainly to question how I expected my 4-hour piano playing and attendance at the American University, with the studying involved, to fit into my social life. The great tempter was Bulent, who had no intention of respecting my new hours. There were some parties we had to attend, such as a cocktail at Aunt Emina Tugay's. Her husband was Turkish Ambassador to Cairo, so it was a pretty formal affair. Princess Faiza was there, as were the three beautiful sultanas, Nesleshah, Hanzade and Nedjla with their husbands. This was not a late affair, so our crowd ended at Faiza's until 4 a.m.

We were now in full holiday season and things were getting really wild: drinks at the Edrey's found everybody in evening dress, so rushed home to

Nawal and Said Toussoun with their son Aziz

change and on to Babs and Eric Tyrell-Martin's. Bulent then forced Faiza, Harry, Johnny Christou, Hassan and me to go to a reception at Cherif Sabry's, the King's uncle. We found "everybody" there from Nahas Pasha, the Prime Minister, to the Chilean Ambassador, the Cattaouis, Omar Pasha Fathy ADC to the King, Serageldine Pasha the Minister of the Interior, Aunt Tugay with her husband the Turkish Ambassador, Ghazali Bey, the Governor of Cairo, Mme Ada Kahil, a great friend of the King's and most of the diplomatic corps and Ali Khan. Rita was sick.

But this was not our idea of fun, so back to the Tyrell-Martins for some dancing. Newly-wed, Sonia Matossian, now the Duchesse de Liancourt, was there with her husband. Sonia and her brother, Jean-Pierre, were our oldest friends, together with Betsey and Jean-Jacques (later Beshara) Takla, whose family owned the *Ahram* newspaper. Our nannies and our parents were friends, but nannies wielded the most power—fearful snobs, they would never allow their charges to frequent unsuitable children, who the children were was more important than friendship between nannies.

The year 1950 ends with a New Year's party at the Auto. There were 500 people there, including His Majesty, more or less officially. Ulvia and I had never been presented to him, so we were not required to greet him. Had we met at a private party, we would have had to make a *temenah* to him. This was a Turkish greeting, you bowed, lowered your right hand towards the ground, then touched your heart and head. The lower you bowed, the more important the person you were greeting. Of course, for the King and Queen, you nearly touched the ground. It beat curtseying, which we found demeaning, although it was much easier to do.

The King's table was next to ours, but no greetings were exchanged. I think he fancied Ulvia, because he threw paper balls at her when Dad was not looking. Dad and HM were on very bad terms.

A word about our evening dresses: Ulvia wore a black velvet top on a white tulle skirt, studded with "diamonds." My dress was ruby red velvet studded with huge "diamonds" ending in a flared, red tulle skirt. The *Musawar*, a popular magazine, devoted about ten pages to photographs of us wearing these gowns as well as various other outfits. Our talent as models cannot honestly be described as anything but awkward. It was not entirely our fault. The photographer had no idea how to take fashion pictures. From our facial expressions you could tell we were annoyed and bored. The photos were in colour, which made things worse. The result, of course, was lamentable.

***

Ali Khan and Rita Hayworth were in town, fêted by everybody. We had a lunch at Hussein Enan Pasha's farm at Marg, just outside Cairo. He was a former Minister of Agriculture and his farm was a showplace.

The verdict on Rita was that "she was very sweet but frightfully shy and ill at ease. He is very amusing, has a great sense of humour." I'm not surprised the poor girl felt ill at ease. She was in an extremely sophisticated and cosmopolitan group of people, who were all acquainted with each other and who used at least three languages in any conversation. Also, she was rather a disappointment looks-wise, as we'd all seen *Gilda* recently, in which she was fabulous. Alaeddin Muchtar, Aunt Emina Tugay's younger brother, was madly in love with Gilda and rather disappointed when he met Rita. It was not so much the lack of beauty, as a lack of sparkle. Her hair was her best feature, but that was not enough. Her face seemed to be greasy, perhaps she was afraid of the strong Egyptian sun! Later on we found out that she was extremely unhappy, that Ali neglected her terribly and was probably unfaithful as well. I find American movie stars unsettling, especially the women. In private, with

Ada Kahil, unidentified person, Princess Fatma Toussoun, Princess Fawzia, Dom João Maria d'Orleans, Nazli Hussein Sabry, Princess Faiza, Dr & Mrs Rashad

few exceptions, they come across as commonplace.

At a dinner hosted by Mohamed Sultan Pasha, one of our most distinguished sportsmen, Ulvia sat next to Princess Ali Khan and could not get more than a word or two out of her. Another time at Jorge's, when he and Carlito were playing guitar, Ali Khan left without a word to his wife. She had to stay until he returned to pick her up. Rita may have been shy, but she soon had enough and we subsequently heard that she'd left him. Then he was sorry, tried to appease her, had a reconciliation of sorts in Paris, but blew it again. Ali Khan was not made for marriage. We saw him at our last Tennis Party in Garden City. He came with a *singer* nobody had ever heard of. But he was always charming. One evening after the revolution we were having dinner with Dad at the Semiramis Grill, where many *old friends* pretended we did not exist. Prince Ali came into the room, saw my father and went up to him immediately, saying "Monseigneur, how pleased I am to see you." Such a gentleman. The last time I saw him was at Longchamps with Nanou. He came up to greet us and Saïd told his wife she should not speak to him because he was dangerous. We replied that he could not seduce us at the races for heaven's sake! Husbands were terrified of him, probably rightly!

***

In early January 1951, I met Ismaïl Hassan. He was Hassan Hassan's elder brother and an occasional recluse. He was a great friend of Uncle Abdallah and Aunt Maria and I met him one afternoon when I joined Bahia, Aleya and their stepmother at the Sporting Club. I went to the movies and then dined at the Izzets, ending at Faiza's, where I found Ismaïl again.

A few days later, Adel called to say they needed me for the film. We shot scenes in the ping-pong room for ages. Then Ismaïl arrived and began to tease

Nevine and Ulvia at Hussein Pasha Enan's farm at Marg

me, trying to pull up my skirt and generally being a pest. He did this with every presentable woman, except Faiza. It was most annoying. He kept trying to kiss me, generally succeeding. I was embarrassed because there were people around.

One time we filmed until 3 a.m. and poor Faiza was sent out of her bedroom because they wanted to film there. Emine and I were bleary-eyed and I got to bed at 4 a.m., cursing the film. Bulent's camera fever had infected Adel and Harry, and we actors were tracked down like preys.

Filming did not exclude seeing the Izzets, Ratibs and the Auto Club crowd. At the Auto, I dined with Mohamed, Loutfia and Abdel Hamid Serageldine, another of Fouad Pasha's brothers. At 11.30, completely foggy on two dry martinis, I went to Zohria. Faiza greeted me enthusiastically, and Ismaïl with kisses galore.

The day before Bahia's wedding, I picked her up and we went to *La Femme nouvelle* to try on her wedding dress. It was gorgeous, white satin with an enormous tulle skirt and train with satin draping ending in a flowing bow at the back. A little white satin bonnet with tulle and lace veil completed the outfit.

On January 25th, the wedding day, I arrived early and went to see the bride. She "looked just lovely, a dream in fact." The guests soon arrived. Prince and Princess Abdel Moneim, Prince and Princess Mohamed Ali Ibrahim, Daddy, the Prime Minister, the Daouds, Fouad Pasha and all the other Serageldines, and Ismaïl. He kept pulling his tongue at me in front of the Serageldines to my great embarrassment. He was absolutely impossible at times and did not care where he was or with whom. I felt like disappearing into the woodwork.

After the wedding, he took me in his car to Faiza's to see new rolls of the film. Then we went to Totes', where it was very boring. Ismaïl and Totes had been great friends for years, and Totes had helped Ismaïl out when he got into a very sticky situation with a prostitute. I don't know the details, but I know Mummy was furious with Totes for years.

Prince Ismail Hassan

I often went to watch polo with Auntie Maria and Aleya, where we saw Archduke Rudolf von Habsburg give the cups away. Wahid Yousry Pasha, the son of Princess Chevikiar and Seifullah Pasha Yousry, was the prime mover in this sport, and his wife, Aunt Samiha, the daughter of Sultan Hussein and Sultana Melek, was very much involved in the polo scene, generally surrounded by a crowd of friends and relations. I thought the Archduke looked awfully thin and pale. Another famous guest was Porfirio Rubirosa, a great polo player.

On to the Izzet house, where the Four Corners is today and where we were always welcome. I loved to sit in the small library in front of a real fire in winter and chat with Uncle and Auntie. They also had very good, light food and I always accepted an invitation to a meal, mostly dinner. We found the brand new Madame Serageldine, sporting a 20 carat diamond ring. We were all green with envy.

Ulvia and I owed a lot of people, so we decided to give a party. Daddy did not, as he wined and dined everybody at the Auto. The house was half empty and to make it look less so was quite a job. Auntie Maria helped me immensely, as I am useless at interior decoration, in fact beware if I offer my services! Daddy did not seem to be enthusiastic about the party and even forgot to order the food and drink. What's more he was in Alex. I called him from the Auto and while I was waiting for the call to come through, Dr. Rashad asked me to have a drink with him and his friends, the Albert Tabets. From the Club, I went to the Wahbas for dinner and then home. Adel picked me up at 11 and we joined Harry and Ismaïl at the Champagne Club. At 12, we went on to Zohria. Ismaïl and I smoked a "cigarette" on the balcony. Of course, he kissed me some more, nearly smothering me.

My party went reasonably well. Nimet and Colette Cattaoui were the first to arrive, followed by the Wahbas as they all lived in Garden City. Faiza came

Nevine, Bahia Izzet and Aunt Maria Izzet at the Guezireh
watching an equestrian event

quite late but was a darling as usual and in high spirits, looking absolutely ravishing as only she could look. People seemed impressed by the house. Dinner was excellent. Afterwards we danced under the staircase.

I seem to have ended up at Zohria almost every evening and very late too. If there were no cars, I did not go in of course. Generally, there were lots of cars, as neither Faiza and certainly not Bulent were early birds. None of us were.

Our next adventure was Upper Egypt. Faiza, Bulent, Emine Muchtar, Johnny Christou and Fayed Sabit were going by train. Ismaïl decided it was idiotic to go by train when you could fly. Dad let me go because Totes' wife, Sonya, agreed to chaperone me. Train or plane, the hours were horrid. Toppy woke me up at 3.30 a.m. and Dad at 4. I staggered out of bed and managed to be ready by 5.15, when Totes arrived. We picked up Sonya, then Ismaïl and Felicity Ingleby-Mackenzie and drove to Almaza. Hugh Fenwick was already in the car with Totes, so I ended on Ismaïl's lap as we were squeezed like sardines. I have a feeling I would have ended on his lap anyway.

The plane took off at 6.30. It was Misrair then, now it's Egyptair. Inside Egypt, flights are frequently at the most ungodly hours. We landed in Luxor about 8, Ismaïl having amused us three girls all the while. We went to the Winter Palace and joined Faiza and Co. for breakfast. Then Ismaïl and I played Harry and Felicity at tennis and lost 2–1, thanks to my dreadful playing. We had lunch with Faiza at 2 and then a rest. I arose at 7.30, had an early dinner and retired at about 10. Ismaïl did not appear at all.

Next day, we went by boat to the opposite bank of the Nile where we visited the Valley of the Kings, Deir el Bahari and looked at the Colossi of Memnon. We met up with some schoolgirls, who according to Bulent said: "There's Nevine Abbas Halim, so sorry she got thinner." Another answered: "So has Princess Faiza." The girls all clapped when Faiza appeared. Lunched in a "shabby little place in a garden," returning at 5.30. Ismaïl joined us for tea.

The following day, we returned to the hotel for lunch, as we were to pay a visit to the Sultana Melek in the afternoon. She had a house in Luxor where she spent most of the winter. It gave onto the Nile with a huge terrace on the roof where she liked to entertain. Faiza and I had to get all dressed up for the visit to our rage. We arrived at exactly 4.40 p.m. and were received by a bevy of elderly ladies. I followed close on Faiza as I had no idea who was a princess and who was a "kalfa" (kind of lady-in-waiting), because they were all dressed the same. The Sultana Melek, widow of Sultan Hussein, awaited us at the top of the stairs. She had been a very beautiful woman and in old age was still lovely and very kind. Princess Vishdan showed me the roof and the garden, in order to leave Princess Faiza alone with the Sultana. We left at 6 or so in a thoroughly bad temper.

After dinner, the others went to a movie. Ismaïl, Felicity, Fayed and I went for a buggy ride. We returned to the salon, and to my surprise Ismaïl was quiet and sensible.

Sonya was feeling ill. Ismaïl persuaded me to get a single room so as not to catch whatever she had. I got her a doctor but she only had an upset stomach. I was now on the same floor as Ismaïl and had to watch my step. Again to my surprise, he behaved like a grown-up. We spent a very quiet evening. I read *Vol de nuit,* with Ismaïl beside me reading *Le Temple dans l'homme.*

We visited Gurna, a model village built of mud bricks. The architect, Hassan Fathy, showed us around himself. It's not every day you get a visit from the King's sister. "I must say I thoroughly enjoyed it, the atmosphere was one of peace and beauty, the air scarcely moving in the hot sun, the green fields stretching towards the foot of the cliffs." We had tea at Hassan Bey's house. We were all very impressed by the concept of Gurna. It was a cheap and salubrious answer to the needs of the fellahin. Unfortunately, the fellahin were not impressed. As soon as they could afford it, they built quite dreadful brick houses, sometimes sticking them onto their mud huts. It's all very well to pity the poor fellah, but he is obstinate and hidebound and it's almost impossible to make him change his habits. It is also extremely difficult to change the habits of the labourers, many of whom of course were former fellahin. At Mahalla al Kubra, there is a huge industrial complex, where the workers are provided with housing. Each family has a couple of rooms, a bathroom and kitchen. I went to visit the various factories and finally we went to see the touted living quarters. Most of the small houses were filthy, filled with chicken, goats, and sometimes even a donkey. The bathroom was the first casualty. The inhabitants, unfamiliar with taps and toilets, broke the taps and clogged the toilets. I'm sorry to say that the only clean streets were the uninhabited ones. The Egyptian is in essence a nice guy, but he is obstinate and will persevere in his way of life no matter what. Cleanliness does not play much of a role in his life, if you have to choose between food and soap... Over the centuries, the fellahin have had many disasters to contend with, from being hauled off their land to work on some government project with no compensation, the *corvée*, to being overtaxed and badly treated by absentee landlords.

The same evening, we were invited to an official dinner by Andraous Pasha. He was a native of Luxor and had a small museum of his own, of which he was justly proud. Princess Faiza was the guest of honour, but Princess Maria-Pia of Italy was also a guest. She was in Luxor chaperoned by a distinguished Italian couple. I went reluctantly, threatened by Bulent if I did not help out Faiza. Bulent also got Johnny Christou to join us, pretending to be a VIP of mysterious origin. Ismaïl had been invited but flatly refused to go. I think Bulent had initially hoped to pass Johnny off as Ismaïl, but realised that there were too many pitfalls. Johnny was a pitfall all by himself. He made me laugh hysterically all evening, while Faiza and Bulent sent me reproachful looks, until Bulent almost succumbed himself. Maria-Pia did! It was an ordeal to get

Sultana Melek

through that dinner without doing something really awful. Our host kept looking at us trying to figure out what the joke was. He showed us his museum after dinner and that precluded any form of hilarity. When the younger daughter played the accordion and sang and then played the piano, we were sorely tried again.

Back at the hotel, Ismaïl was none too happy to find out that Johnny and I had had a hilarious time at the dinner party. With hindsight, it would seem that Ismaïl was falling in love with me. I was much too stupid to realise this, even when he told me that if he were a marrying man he'd marry me. I had no desire to marry at all, and thought him both rude and condescending to even mention it. I've always been emotionally retarded and very proud in spite of having an inferiority complex. Ismaïl was beginning to treat me like his private property, while giving me no hope for the future. I resented this and being a spoilt brat, I began to play the field.

I was careful never to flirt with somebody else when he was around, because I'd done that on one memorable occasion and the scene he made scared me to death. It obviously did not scare me enough, because during the International Tennis Championships I went to a party for the tennis players at the Auberge with Budge Patty. For my bad luck, Ismaïl was at the Véronique, the nightclub part of the Auberge, and he saw me leave with Budge. I was only giving Budge a lift back to his hotel, but I must admit that it was severe provocation. After that, it was over for Ismaïl and he would have nothing more to do with me. When it was too late, I realised my stupidity. However, thinking of what marriage to him would have been like, I realise that it would never have worked. I was much too spoilt and stupid, and he suffered from severe depressions on and off. I did not have the maturity or depth of understanding to have kept the marriage going. And it's I who would have had to do most of the work.

We are still in Luxor and all is rosy. We took the boat to Dendera, one of the best preserved temples of Ptomainic times and spent a while inspecting it. On our return to the Winter Palace, we found Sonya and Ismaïl waiting to have tea with us. We had another fight and he swore he'd rape me. I was petrified. Of course, he was only kidding but I was naïve and stupid. He was a decent person even if he cheated at cards and had fits of fury. After dinner, I read while the others played cards. He followed me to my room and forced me to show him my diary, kissed me and left. Then he peeped through the keyhole of my bathroom and said I was not at all bad naked. I was livid with rage and deeply humiliated.

Next day, we visited the temple of Karnak. Its restoration was being done by Mr. Chévrier who showed us around. Afterwards, Faiza, Bulent, Emine and I were invited to lunch at the Sultana Melek's, where we had to eat an enormous amount of food. Then Bulent, Emine and I were told to sit in one corner of the garden while the Sultana and Faiza had a chat. I wondered what the Sultana had to say in confidence, if she knew how dangerous the political situation was. None of us realised what was happening. Demonstrations, assassinations, bombs in cinemas, riots, so what?

After the visit to the Sultana, we played tennis. Harry and I had a spat and I banged my nose in the door and yelled with rage, while Sonya and Ismaïl tried to calm me down. Ismaïl and I dined with friends of his, the Bekhyts, René Toriel and Miss Shiha, while the others went to a village festival. Later, he and I played patience. He came to kiss me goodnight later. What more could a girl want?

On our return to Cairo, things were different. We were no longer practically living together. We met at the Sporting or at Zohria, but it was not the same. We did adjust and everybody was helping the affair along. One evening at the Scarabée, Ismaïl went into the bar and finding HM there, he said "Good evening, Your Majesty." The King was very fond of Ismaïl, had given him the title of prince, even though there already was a Prince Hassan, and rightly assessing his condition, laughingly replied and waved him away. I was hiding behind the door, not wanting HM to see me. We knew that the King was well informed on what we were all up to. He kept a close watch on his sisters and would arrive at their houses unannounced, to check up on them personally. This happened one evening when we were all at Faiza's. General panic, with the rest of us all disappearing into the garden, leaving Faiza and Bulent to face the music by themselves. He did not stay long and they told us he was perfectly amiable. He must have seen all our cars in the driveway and his minions would have told him exactly who they belonged to.

I met Ismaïl's Spanish mother for tea with the Izzets at the Club. She was the reason her children did not automatically receive titles on birth. Even a prince had to marry a born Moslem. It was Princess Nimet Muchtar, King Fouad's sister, who pleaded with him to give the girls, Hadidja and Aicha, titles so that they could find decent husbands. But it was King Farouk who gave titles to the boys. I liked Madame Hassan very much—no title for her, poor dear. I don't think she cared much either. She would have been a great mother-in-law, but probably quite unable to deal with Ismaïl. He was very proud of his Spanish side, every summer was spent in Spain at the Costa Brava, the only beach not ruined by tourists he would say. We were very curious to know what he did there. He always went to the same place, but never described it or mentioned the people he met. Imagine being married to that?

I'm dragging out the good parts. He took me to his sister Hadidja's in Maadi, where we found the usual crowd. On the way home, he said I had behaved like a *putain*. This did not prevent us from meeting at Faiza's the next evening to watch the films we made in Luxor. Tickling me as usual, he lifted me off my feet and kissed me. "I do not understand why he cannot be gentle. His brusqueness makes me hysterical and I hate to be poked at and tickled." Then Sonia told me that everybody was talking about Ismaïl and me. "Well, they can go shoot. I will not be trapped for ages!" A few weeks later, I would have given my soul to be trapped by him.

At the Tyrell-Martin's party, he made a furious scene because I danced with Victor Simeika, who apart from being a friend of my parents was also their age. Then an Arabic paper published something about Ismaïl and me. Here, my inferiority complex and pride entered. I was terribly excited by the rumours, but Ismaïl had been so definite about not getting married, that my pride made me hostile and I behaved like an untamed colt. I don't think Ismaïl had ever been really in love before, anyhow not with somebody eligible. His marriage to Sousou Yehia had been arranged and did not last. When I met him, his love life consisted of hookers and he made no secret of it. I was not shocked, although at first I found his language awful. I don't know why, considering Daddy's was much the same and often worse.

Ulvia and I saw very little of each other, so we decided to have lunch and go to the movies together. Later François, the best coiffeur in Egypt according to us, did our hair. François had his salon next to the Auto Club and I spent lots of time there, as my hair frizzed at the slightest hint of dampness. He was married to the mother of one of our best jockeys, Angelo Jr., who was killed in a racing accident. Really awful. The Ratibs, who owned race horses and hence knew all the jockeys, told us about it. A very stupid, unlucky fall!

At a formal party at Zohria, Ulvia wore her new black and white dress and I my ruby one. We arrived early as requested by Bulent. Sousou, Ismaïl and Harry were already there. I was not speaking to Ismaïl, but later Harry and Irène Catseflis forced us to make up. We danced and he took me home at 4.30 a.m.

Aunt Hadidja, mother of my six Halim aunts, who had been married to Prince Abbas Halim, Dad's uncle, died on February 22nd. After a visit of condolence at Aunt Hadidja's house in Helwan, where we found two of her daughters, Aunts Tewfika and Emina, we went to Granny's. She was tired and very sad. Then to Aunt Kerima's, who lived in Maadi. A very sad day. It was when I met Tewfik Toussoun.

Two days later, Harry and I drove over to Zohria, having met at the Sporting. We found Bulent looking glum, Ismaïl showed up and then Faiza appeared. We all went to Hassan's for drinks, then back to Zohria, piling into Ismaïl's car. On arrival, Ismaïl and Saleh Sabit had a fight, Bulent and Johnny quarrelled, then things got really bad and Faiza and Bulent had a fight. I don't know why everybody's nerves were shot. Ulvia and I looked on, but did not dare intervene. Then Ismaïl kissed me to show Ulvia "how." Thankfully things did finally calm down and we all went home for much-needed sleep.

Things were still going well with Ismaïl, even if we quarrelled a lot. One day, Ismaïl took Harry and me to his flat at the Immobilia. I remember it as pretty awful, all in browns, not a single piece of decent furniture, like a cheap furnished flat. I had no idea what Ismaïl's financial situation was. He bought a new car, was decently dressed, and coughed up when we went out. He went to Spain every summer. His brother Hassan, who must have had the same, possibly less, had a beautiful flat in Garden City full of valuable furniture, carpets, etc. Hassan was an artist and cared for lovely objects, whereas Ismaïl seemed supremely uninterested. That would have been a plus had we married, because as an interior decorator I was a disaster. We would not have lived in his flat, of course, so there would have had to be decoration of the new apartment or house. I'm not surprised he had attacks of acute depression, anybody living in that horrible apartment would have. The Immobilia was a frightfully depressing place to begin with, an enormous grey building like a prison. It's main advantage was that it was anonymous and lots of people had *garconnières* there. There were several entrances and the place was like a

Nevine, Zoë Reese, Fred Kovaleski, Budge Patty, Dick Savitt, Ulvia at the RACE

beehive, with lifts here and there and to get to your destination you needed the bawab's help, which was given with palm outstretched.

Looking through my diary, I see that we all drank like Cossacks from whom we are supposedly descended on the female side. It occurred to me that the King was extremely lenient towards Ulvia and me, considering that he met us almost every night in some night spot or other and that we were not married. As Head of the Family, he could very well have told Dad to rein us in. Thank heavens he did not, perhaps he felt the day of reckoning was not far off.

We are reaching the end of the story. Ismaïl decided to go to Italy to see an important football match. I don't know why I took this as a personal insult, and when he decided to sleep instead of living it up with Fayed and me until his plane left at 5 a.m., I was fearfully hurt and rushed to see Bulent to tell him about it. Princess Fawzia was there and I could only see him in the hall for a few minutes. I went home and cried bitterly. Looking back, I cannot understand why I was in such a state. I often did not see him for days, so why the fuss about this trip?

The International Tennis Tournaments were starting and we met all the stars. Mohamed Sultan gave a cocktail party at the RACE for the players. Zoë was invited and spent all evening stuck to Budge Patty, who had just won Wimbledon. Later we went on to the Semiramis and he managed to get "unstuck." Every afternoon saw us at the tennis matches. The King's sisters with their husbands had the Royal loge and we the President's box, although we often sat on the benches with our non-royal friends. It was more fun as we didn't have to sit like graven images. There were cocktail and dinner parties almost every night. Important matches had to be taken into consideration, and as the semi-finals and finals approached, the boys had to go back to the hotel relatively early. At the Camara cocktail, Sonia told me people were saying that we girls were chasing the tennis players.

*Nevine with Mohamed Sultan Pasha, Countess Yolande de Zogheb
and Gottfried von Cramm*

Despite the frenzy, I managed to lunch at Granny's. Auntie Mi was staying with her; we'd not met since Switzerland, twelve years before. She was still a darling and looked great.

Ismaïl was back from Italy on March 6 and phoned me on arrival. Budge had invited me to dinner the day before and after having tea with Ismaïl and Harry at the Club, I went home to dress for my date. We dined at Khomais and went on to the Auberge, where we saw a very bad show.

I lunched at the RACE with Ismaïl and then we went to the tennis. I took Budge to the Auberge to join the other players and met Ismaïl as we were leaving. He was drunk, abusive and angry. I had not yet realised that this was the end as far as Ismaïl was concerned. He had never asked about my other groups and his jealousy was only aroused when he could see what I was doing.

Then, Budge invited Ulvia out. I was mortified and richly deserved it. Here I was throwing a great man away because of this two-timer. My involvement with Ismaïl was anything but solid, and I did have a crush on Patty. This makes me sick and I want to get to the end of this sorry period.

Budge continued to flirt with me but obviously preferred Ulvia. At the Tyrell-Martins, he and I got very drunk, but it was Ulvia who drove him to Zohria and later took him back to his hotel.

The finals were on Sunday, March 11th, also our Tennis Party at Garden City. There were over 200 guests and it was a great success. Faiza did not come as she was not feeling well. Ismaïl, pretending he was sick, did not come either. I was beginning to understand how foolish I'd been.

There was a lunch at the Semiramis with the Adrian Conan-Doyles (she was a Georgian princess, he a cousin of Sherlock Holmes' creator), Budge Patty, Ali Khan, Ulvia, an English poet and an Indian tennis player with his wife. A waiter brought Budge a cable. That's when we found out his real name: Gaius! It was a wire from Barbara Hutton wishing him Happy Birthday.

Tennis tournament at the Guezireh, 1951
Nevine towards the end of the first row, behind her Prince Abbas Halim, Field
Marshal Montgomery in the middle of the second row

It was the rest period between the Cairo and Alexandria tennis tournaments. I called Ismaïl who sounded really sick. The Izzets, his mother and I went to see him. "He looked very unhappy, but not too ill. He was not his usual talkative self, but now and then he offered a few characteristic remarks. I think he is still very peeved with me or perhaps it's just over. Well, we'll soon see."

I saw a lot of Salah el Orabi at that time. We played tennis and he often joined us at the Sporting. He was a good tennis player and sometimes sent me some balls that nearly killed me. We continued the usual round until we left for Alex and the tournament there. At the Alexandria Sporting, we met Fred, Dick and Budge, who took us to the cocktail party for the tennis players at the Golf House where we saw lots of our friends. Later a large group of us went to La Petite Hutte, Costia Mitarachi's place, just our style." Ul scorned Budge and talked to Piero Verbinshak, so Budge and I talked together." I took him back to the Windsor hotel.

Next day, I waited for Dad to go to the tennis, and therefore arrived very late. I saw von Cramm and Davidson smother Cernik and Drobny. I later gave them the "Coupe des Nations." We drank champagne to celebrate Lena's birthday, dined at the Petit Coin de France and ended at La Petite Hutte. It was very dull and we were all in a bad mood. Exhaustion most likely.

The following day there was tea at Nanou's. Budge and I went to the Union for dinner and then to the movies. I wondered why Budge had asked me out. Next day, he was all over Ulvia. I was at the Catseflis where I found the Stagnis, de Jenners, Dimitri, and later Faiza and finally the Charles Reeses arrived.

Next I lunched at the Toussouns, picked up Faiza to go to the tennis and watched Patty and von Cramm beat Cucelli and Del Bello in three straight sets. Then Savitt and Drobny beat Kovaleski and Dorfman hollow. Princess Faika was there too, with her tennis-playing husband.

It rained next day and nobody knew if they could play, but finally at

*Fawzia, Fouad Sadek, Ismail Cherine, Faika, Faiza, Bulent Raouf and Ulvia,
watching tennis*

3.30 p.m. they did. Savitt and Drobny beat Patty and von Cramm with great difficulty in five sets. That evening I broke the last straw on the camel's back: I drove Budge back to Cairo alone in my car. Nanou told me later that Ismaïl had been horrified by this.

The tennis men were gone and we returned to our usual amusements. I had lunch at the RACE and Ismaïl turned up, but sat miles away and we were both icy. I played tennis then went to Zohria where the whole group arrived and we dined at the Hermitage and ended at the Helmia, where Faiza, Bulent and Hassan turned up. Annie Berrier was a "protégée" of HM and at the Scarabée sang "La Chanson du Nil", especially for him. She had a nice voice, low and husky.

Life continued with tennis lessons, the Sporting, and Zohria. Ismaïl was at the Sporting. He soon left to go home to bed and we did not speak. Sonya thinks I gave him a very good lesson. "Personally I do not know whether he is furious or indifferent. He cannot be indifferent, because if he were he'd act normally and he is in a foul mood these days – perhaps it's something else."

The end of the love affair had come. I woke up to reality at last, tried everything, and everybody helped me, but Ismaïl would have nothing more to do with me. He was very polite, but there was no way of shaking him. Human nature being what it is, I naturally never wanted anybody as much as I wanted him. He was my Great Love. I must add that I never suffered with respect to a love affair as I did with him. Until then, I was always the one to leave. This was a new experience. The fact that if the affair had continued, it would either end in marriage or a break, and the realisation that marriage to Ismaïl would have been a disaster, did not console me. He was a very complex and private person, never revealing his "innermost self." He had been a fighter pilot in the first war against Israel and Hassan told us that during the great cholera epidemic, he worked with the peasants in Upper Egypt. But he could spend months locked up in his flat at the Immobilia. He listened to operatic music for hours, often playing the same aria countless times. When he emerged, he would really live it up. After our break-up, he retired for a time. In the summer he went to Spain as usual.

In the fall, I tried one last time to speak to Ismaïl and he agreed that I could visit him. He kissed me passionately, but when he tried to rape me, I left. He must have thought I'd been to bed with scores of men and that now, I'd be willing. He made one revealing and devastating remark to Adel, who repeated it to me much later, that he had never intended to let matters go so far. That was the end for me!

Sorrowfully, we moved from Garden City to a temporary flat in Rue Maspero, while our apartments on Kamel Mohamed Street in Zamalek were being decorated by Edmond Soussa, painter turned interior decorator. I had decorated the Maspero flat myself. I went to Salon Vert, the best shop for household materials, and bought emerald green moiré to cover a sofa, two armchairs and a few curtains. Once this was all in place, you felt queasy, in fact quite bilious I was informed. To make matters worse, we were on the last floor and the windows and doors being badly fitted, the wind would roar in, moving the ghastly curtains and smothering you in an emerald cloud.

* * *

Summer of 1951 was the last summer before the revolution. We remained in Cairo until the beginning of June and continued the usual rounds. Aicha Hassan, Ismaïl's younger sister gave a dinner at which I arrived very late, at 10.30 p.m. to find Madame Hassan, the rest of the Hassan family, Princess Faika, Annamaria Edrey, etc. I drank martinis galore and felt rather dizzy. Ismaïl was there and even said hello to me, "but when I talked to him later, he said he was mad with nobody, but not going out these days, did not sit with me at the Club, because of the people I was with – a lot of bosh." They were the same people he sat with when I was at another table. It is strange how a basically decent person can become a sadist once he or she has the upper hand.

With Faiza, Adel, Evie, Saleh and Hassan we went to have our fortunes told by a sheikh in Khan Khalil, through which we walked in a "wonderful atmosphere of mystery and beauty."

The Berlin Philharmonic conducted by Furtwängler played at the Rivoli Haydn's "Horloge Symphony", R. Strauss' "Tod und Verklärung" and Beethoven's 7th Symphony. I liked the last piece best. Princesses Faiza, Faika, Neslesháh and Hanzade were in the audience, "beautiful and resplendent as ever."

A short trip to Alex in April, mainly to try on my dress for the King's wedding at Solange's. We were invited to Ali Pasha Yehia's house to see the room he had dedicated exclusively to miniature trains, with stations, bridges, tunnels, etc. We met his beautiful young wife, Itir, for the first time. We were to see them at various parties and duly admired her magnificent jewels.

In Cairo on May 5th, I met Ismaïl at the RACE and later at the Sporting. He even took me to Zohria in his car. I went to Amin Sedky's cocktail party with Dad and Yolande. Ismaïl was there and he took me home at midnight. Attitude very distant.

Next day was the King's wedding. I lunched at the Auto with the Amin Sedkys, Dad, Yolande and Ulvia. At 3.30 I went home to dress, helped by Ulvia and Yolande. The dress was white silk with embroidered white flowers and sequins glittering here and there and a small train. It was worn with an ice-blue satin coat, long white gloves and a *yashmak*. Yolande lent me her sapphire earrings, broach and bracelet, which went well with the coat. The ice-blue satin coat was perfect and Yolande's sapphires enhanced the dress. Then there was the small embroidered cap of the yashmak to hold the lower part,

Nevine, Ulvia, Shehriar, Djehanquir, Djidji and Annamaria Edrey

generally with pearl-topped pins. Once in the Palace, this part was removed, so it had to be done easily.

I got to Abdine Palace before 5 p.m. and was taken to the ladies waiting room by one of the King's chamberlains. I was greeted by a cold stare from the ladies, except for Nanou. I went to sit with her and also spoke to Aicha Hassan, Aunt Shahira, who was married to the King's maternal uncle, and Aunt Adila, the wife of Prince Soliman Daoud. Finally, we went into an enormous hall, with the King and the new Queen standing on one side and the rest of the Royal Family and diplomatic corps on the other. We shook hands and did a *temenah* to both and moved on. After the Royal Family, the ladies of the diplomatic corps were presented, then the Queen's family, Court officials, and ministers' wives.

We had tea. I talked to Bulent, Ismaïl, Hassan and Prince Mohamed Ali (still the Crown Prince), and met the Agha Khan and the Begum. She was beautiful and charming. The Royal Family was then herded together to take the obligatory photograph. You can see part of my face if you know where to look. I went home with Dad. The crowds cheered him as we drove by.

One May morning, I awoke feeling awful with a temperature of 39 and returned to bed. Ulvia brought Dr. Rashad over who said I had the grippe. Then Dad arrived with Dr. Abbas, "who made the same astounding discovery." Lots of visitors made a great deal of noise and I felt even hotter. "Dr. Rashad phoned to say I should take six Aspros, Dr. Abbas had said three were enough. Nothing like the medical profession to give you confidence." Next day, in the bathroom I felt very weak, managed to unlock the door and fainted completely. Dr. Rashad arrived and gave me an injection and new medicines. I had more guests, Jackie Djeddah and Pierre Zarpanelly, who were very rowdy and my temperature went up again. Ismaïl and Saleh called to ask how I was.

Mum arrived next day. She was at the Semiramis with Mr. Rediker. Great

The Royal Family at the wedding of King Farouk and Nariman

joy and excitement but there I was stuck in bed. Finally, I went to see her two days later. She "looked fine, fresh and lovely as ever if a little tired owing to the heat." Mr. Rediker turned up and at 8.30, Dad and Uncle Abdallah arrived. Dad, none too happy with the situation, made barbed remarks to Mr. Rediker.

May 17th was Faiza and Bulent's wedding anniversary. I got up early to find a present for them. I found lovely Saxe bowls at Au Seize, had them filled by Groppi and sent to Zohria. Ulvia and I showed up at 10, coming from the Auto. We found lots of people at Faiza's: Zoë, Hassans, Assems, Jojo, Annamaria, etc. and Ismaïl was full of beans.

At a cinema, saw the "Actualités" of the Royal Wedding, with Dad and Ismaïl walking down the steps of Koubbeh Palace laughing, obviously making obscene jokes. The ceremony must have taken place at Koubbeh, with men only, because we went to Abdine for the reception.

Mum decided to leave after barely ten days. She said she could not stand it. I don't know what she was hoping for, arriving with a new husband, she could scarcely hope Dad would murder him and take her back! It seems Totes had been with them on the Semiramis Roof the night before and had insulted Mum, Dad and Rediker. That was pretty good going, even for Totes.

I didn't seem overly affected by Mum's departure. She did manage to worm the Ismaïl story out of me. She thought he must have "cared a great deal to break off so brutally." That was no consolation and it had made me feel worse than I'd felt in some time.

So I went riding with Luis Perinat at the Pyramids. He was being fought over by Samiha and Zoë, Sam being in possession at the moment. But Zozo is very dangerous! I don't know why we went off together, probably for a little peace and quiet, both being in a mess and wanting to forget it.

On June 2nd, we all left for Alex. In spite of my ruined love life, I didn't seem worried about not keeping an eye on Ismaïl. What I do is contract mumps! That put me on the side lines for a while and by the time I emerged, Ismaïl had left for Spain.

This summer, lots of our friends were travelling. Had Ismaïl been around, it would not have meant anything. There is only so much suffering you can cling to when you are 21 years old in a group full of attractive, unattached young men. My new love was Raouf Abousbah, a distant cousin. His mother and mine were second cousins. I'd been miserable long enough and, although once in a while I sighed for what might have been, I did not waste too much time crying in a corner. Raouf was in another group, which consisted mainly of his brothers and sister and the Ratibs.

On September 9th, Ulvia got engaged to the youngest Ratib, Shehriar. The eldest brother, Djehanquir and his wife Djehane called Djidji, came to fetch me and we went to the Auto to see Dad to request his permission for the marriage. This he gave with great pleasure as he knew and liked Shehriar very much, as did we all. Of course, the Palace had to agree too, but no problem as the Ratibs are a distinguished family with ties to the Royal Family through the Daouds and the Yeghens. Ulvia and Shehriar then visited Granny. Everything went well and when Ali and I arrived later, she gave us a very amusing account of it. Granny was very strict as far as behaviour was concerned, but she had a wicked sense of humour and would often surprise us with her perspicacity.

On September 15th, I left for Cairo with Toppy and Sambo. On the way, we saw a dreadful accident, the parents of screaming children seemed in a terrible state. Dad told us never to touch wounded people as we could do more harm than good, but to send for professional help. At the Rest House, we sent an ambulance to the site, without much hope for the adults in the accident. Dad had been trying for years to have that death trap of a desert road made into a two-way auto route. It took quite a few more years until it was finally done. In the meantime, Dad had had a bad accident on it and Gottfried von Cramm killed himself. The accidents occurred mostly when some halfwit tried passing without seeing what was coming in the opposite direction; lots of hills concealed the oncoming cars. Then there were the vehicles left at the side of the road without signs or lights. Most of the time they were huge lorries and running into one of them was fatal. Dad had run into a huge Egyptair container and sued them. After the revolution, of course, he could not win.

Drama entered our lives. Raouf's father, Saleh Abousbah was accused of killing his cousin, a Yeghen, father of Rukia, the wife of Ilhami Ratib, first cousin to Shehriar. He was accused of assassinating him on his farm, because the body was found in a canal. Saleh Bey was the least likely suspect one could imagine. He was not very tall, slim and a very quiet and courteous man. Needless to say, he was cleared, but it took an unreasonably long time and he remained in jail for what seemed ages.

I saw a lot of Samiha Khayatt, a member of the Zohria group. We met at the beach or at the Auto. One evening I had dinner at her house, and her mother told us about the rehabilitation of prostitutes and the third degree used by the police to get confessions from criminals. Hassan Hassan in his book mentions the social work carried out by "society ladies", who did a great deal of good without any publicity. Their modesty and devotion precluded any fanfare. Winnie Khayatt, Samiha's mother, was one of those ladies.

Back in Cairo to register at the American University, I stayed with Bahia and Zaki Serageldine. They had an enormous and very beautiful apartment in Zamalek. She was pregnant and we ate huge meals and the following day I did not even dress. Zaki must have been away, because I did not know him well enough to slouch around in pyjamas in his presence.

On September 24th, our paternal grandfather, Prince Ibrahim Halim, died and Dad returned to Cairo for the funeral. Grandpa had a State Funeral as the

Labour celebrating Prince Abbas Halim's return from hospital after his accident on the desert road

The funeral of Prince Ibrahim Halim

last grandson of Mohamed Ali the Great. It was the last State Funeral before the revolution.

**

Our summer lifestyle continued until October 3rd when I returned to Cairo to enter University. Our new flats were not yet ready, so Toppy and I installed ourselves at the Semiramis Hotel. I seem to have overlooked the fact that some classes started at 8 a.m. Bulent and Faiza were still away, but Raouf was not.

For the formalities, I only had to appear at 11.30. And surprise! The Dean of Women is none other than Wadad Habib, the grad student I'd met at Bryn Mawr. I'm also in her Philosophy class. She introduced me to Suzy Habashy and Djenane Kamel, whose brother Cherif I knew very well. I also met Dora Doss (later she changed her name to Shahira) and Francine Behman.

The second week bode none too well for the future. I was out every evening, mostly with Raouf and Co. and never got to bed before midnight. On my first Saturday, we ended at the Auberge and later Véronique and I got to bed at 5 a.m. I started cutting classes as early as October 17th, when I was too tired to go to my Economics class. In my defence, I must add that I found Economics and Sociology horribly dry and boring. I managed to pass by just reading the summaries at the end of each chapter. I never had the time or patience to read all of it. Philosophy was pretty confusing, English a bore and we had a Psychology teacher with a horrific accent, who generally made us hysterical with laughter. I felt much less amused when I had to give a lecture on the "Eye" in Physiology. I'd rashly opted to give an oral rather than a written description of the eye. As usual, I'd not gone to much trouble and had only made a few notes, not realising that orally I needed much more input to fill the allotted ten minutes. I came to the end of my masterly speech in no time, and my fellow students were then allowed to ask questions. My pals abstained, but the stupidest boy in the class came up with a few nasty ones. I could not answer them and looked at our teacher with despair and bless him, he thanked me and I could sit down. But I learnt a very salutary lesson.

At AUC, they had none of the subjects I'd taken at Bryn Mawr, except English Literature and Philosophy. I could choose to major in either Sociology or Journalism. I would have loved the latter, but as a member of the Royal Family it was out of the question that I work as a journalist. The kind of journalism I had in mind was to be a "Political Commentator", trying to work out what was really going on in the world behind the wads of bull served us with breakfast. It's probably safer not to know as there have been suspicious disappearances of people who were too curious.

Then we are off to Alex to attend the Mediterranean Games. I went with Dad, sat with Princess Fawzia, her husband Ismaïl Cherine and Queen Geraldine of Albania. The latter was so kind and pretty. Egypt beat Spain 41-39 at basketball, a terrific match. I left the exalted company and rejoined my friends. We all ended at the Pergola and bed was at 3 a.m.

In Economics, our teacher known as "Mac" gave us "a futile lecture on the uninteresting development of the salamander. What it has to do with our course is beyond all of us." Another time, he spoke of the "palpitations of the heart." That finished him! Poor Mac, he was a very nice guy. That's why I guess.

My hours being what they now were, in spite of cutting classes, I saw a lot more of Ulvia's group. Most of them were also university students. Hashem and Hisham Mooro, sons of one of our leading surgeons, were following in their father's footsteps. Mahmoud Soliman, a relative of Hussein Pasha Sirry the on and off PM was studying law. There was Mahmoud Erfan who married one of Ulvia's best friends, Nichole Shiha. Their daughter later married and divorced the only son of President Sadat. We were all invited to the wedding which took place in the garden of President Sadat's house in Giza. It was just after his return from the Camp David peace agreement and we gave him a standing ovation as he walked to his table.

At AUC, they had the revolting habit of "initiating" newcomers and to show I was a good sport I had to go through with it. We put on our oldest jeans and T-shirts and were led into the cellar of AUC's principal building. We were made to crawl through several dark rooms all the while being pelted with sawdust and macaroni. It was not too terrible, but our aspect afterwards was disgusting. I was living at the Semiramis, the most elegant and luxurious hotel in Cairo, and although I snuck in a side door and went up in a side lift, people in the lobby could see me only too well. There was one lady, a resident at the hotel and one of the worst gossips in Cairo, who always sat in the same chair from which she commanded a view of all the entrances to the hotel. Of course, she was at her usual place when I tried to sneak in and soon I was the unwilling victim of a mystery.

I was quite a curiosity at AUC because I was the only female member of the Royal Family at university. With Dad as President of the RACE, one journalist interviewed me about cars and traffic. We discussed jeeps and I remember making a few idiotic remarks about service vehicles, comparing the various makes. There was also a photo of me standing beside a jeep in the grounds of AUC. As if that were not enough, I had to deal with nasty remarks from my fellow students about the current running of the country. They were extremely critical, some were communists, others seemed more like anarchists. If we'd all known what was ahead, I'm sure we would have clung tooth and nail to the present.

Both 1950 and 1951 were bad years for us and for Egypt. In 1950, we were back to the old problems of the Wafd in power and the British refusing to leave. The King, on November 16th, 1950, insisted that all British troops immediately evacuate the Suez Canal zone and the Sudan. The Foreign Secretary, Ernest Bevin, told Parliament that British troops would remain in the Sudan until Egypt and Britain modified the existing treaty mutually; the key word being "mutually." A month later, the Egyptian Foreign Minister discussed the revision of the Treaty with Bevin, but negotiations dragged on.

Women demanded the right to vote. The Wafd introduced a bill in Parliament proposing a right to vote for all women over 21. The King ordered the distribution of Crown domains to landless peasants, but the only mention of it was claimed by the Wafd government.

In August 1951, Egypt revoked the Treaty with Britain. In October, Great Britain refused the unilateral revocation of the treaty and warned Egypt that she would not withdraw her troops from the Suez Canal. France, the US, Turkey and Britain suggested a defence system for the Middle East, with Egypt responsible for the Suez Canal. Egypt refused. A few days later, the Egyptian Parliament approved the abrogation of the Anglo-Egyptian Treaty of 1936 and King Farouk took the title of King of Egypt and the Sudan. Confrontations between Egyptian police and British soldiers left twelve dead, mostly Egyptians.

In November, Egypt and Great Britain agreed that British troops would withdraw from the three major cities of the Canal, Ismailia, Suez and Port Saïd. This did not prevent a six-week strike in Suez by Egyptian dockers and more fighting between British soldiers and Egyptian civilians, with sixteen dead and sixty wounded, mostly Egyptians. It was at this time that the Egyptian Minister of Social Affairs, Abdel Fattah Hassan Pasha sent a telegram to the Director General of the International Labour Office in Geneva, accusing the British military in the Canal zone of consistently mistreating Egyptian workers and arresting a number of Egyptian police officers and interning them. The ILO sent the telegrams to the British government which denied all allegations and accused the Egyptian government of the same crimes.

Egypt recalled its Ambassador to Great Britain in protest at the intervention of the British Army in the Suez Canal. On 6 January 1952, 3500 employees of the Suez Canal Co. went on strike, and the town of Suez was surrounded by the British Army. There was more fighting when Egyptian commandos attacked the British garrison at Tel el Kebir. General Erskine, the British CinC, demanded they surrender in two hours. The Egyptians were ordered to resist and sixty were killed. On January 25th, Ismaïlia was the site of serious confrontations between the British Army and Egyptian police. Among the policemen who refused to give up their arms, 46 were killed, 72 wounded and 800 taken prisoner.

Next day in Cairo, January 26th, was "Black Saturday." It began with a general strike at all factories, with students from the Universities of Fouad, Ibrahim and El-Azhar joining with the workers arriving from the periphery and all converging towards the centre of town. From the PM's balcony, Abdel-Fattah Hassan, State Minister, harangued the crowd, promising immediate breaking off of all ties with Great Britain and the conclusion of a Treaty of Friendship with the USSR.

But it was just before noon that the arsonists began their work. Who organised it? And why? To get rid of the King, of the British, of other foreigners? It was not Mr. Jefferson Caffery or his "boys." He was far too stupid. And he reaped what he sowed, from his "boys", who were such "good boys."

Foreigners, mainly British, were murdered and the police did nothing, supposedly overwhelmed. The King was entertaining the heads of the Army and Police for lunch at Abdine Palace. The story goes that he asked Haydar Pasha what was going on. The reply was there was nothing to worry about, although the head of the political police, Ibrahim Imam, could not be found. Did the King believe him? It was only late afternoon when the Army finally put an end to the carnage. In the meantime, most of inner Cairo was burning.

I'd been scheduled to lunch with a friend and go to the movies and was driving towards the restaurant when I saw a crowd of people running towards me. One man told me to go home as the cinemas were being burnt. I went to the RACE instead as the bridges were blocked, and Sambo took my car to safety. To my relief, I found Daddy at the Club and thanks to him the Club was not burnt. He went down into the street twice and threatened to burn with the Club if they set fire to it. They recognised him as the Labour leader, cheered him and let us be. Another strange thing. A mob bent on destruction does not generally make exceptions.

Stories circulated as to why the rampage was allowed to go on for so long and why the police did nothing. Some guessed it was a duel between the Palace and the Wafd government. Fouad Serageldine, who was Minister of the Interior, knew what was going on but did nothing. The King must have thought it an excellent occasion to get rid of the hated Wafd, which he promptly did next day, firing Nahas, who was "unable to keep order and guarantee security" and appointing Ali Maher Pasha as Prime Minister. The entire Diplomatic Corps protested against the riots of "Black Saturday." Obviously they thought it was a stratagem and did not relish being the guinea pigs.

From that day on, things became more and more unreal. The King and the Wafd were playing a dangerous game, from which neither would escape.

First we had a curfew from 10 p.m. to 6 a.m., later from 11 p.m. The parties continued, only now you had to decide whether to go home early or spend the night. We were dancing on the extreme edge of the abyss, and like all the other times in history, we refused to look the situation in the face, or wherever else one looks situations in.

Another strange thing was the concentrated campaign of hatred against the King. The worst he was accused of was corruption and surrounding himself with an unsavoury group of sycophants, who profited from their nearness to the King. Even so, corruption in Egypt is endemic. Of course, one would prefer if the King were not accused of corruption, especially as he did not need it. He did whatever he liked, anyway. Egyptians are a cynical lot and if he'd been more energetic in combating his bad image, he'd still be king. Going to nightclubs and running after girls was no crime. He never drank alcohol and never ate pork. As for the girls, Moslem men are allowed four wives and women are still considered second class citizens. The general public certainly did not blame him for his women. They did sense, however, that he seemed not to care about his people and his country, that he purposely made himself unpopular. He capped all this with supposedly falling in love with a young girl, Nariman Sadek, already engaged to a respectable lawyer, Zaki Hashem, and deciding to marry her himself. This went down badly with everybody, from the Royal Family to the man in the street.

I again went to his wedding, but as a grown-up and in a very different social climate. There was no rejoicing and no cheers in the streets. The King and his new bride honeymooned in Europe and he was shown spending huge amounts of money and gambling in all the well-known casinos. A year later, Nariman produced the much desired heir, Ahmed Fouad. No rejoicing then either and six months later, King Farouk abdicated at the age of 32. In the space of ten years, he had managed to go from a beloved, handsome young monarch to a bloated, cynical man, looking twenty years older than his age.

All his biographers, whether critical or unbiased, say it was such a shame. But he had a great deal against him.

His mother seemed to take pleasure in embarrassing him. She went off to America, taking her two youngest daughters with her. One of the girls, Faika, married Fouad Sadek, a member of her mother's entourage and returned to Egypt. The youngest, Fathia, married a Copt, who murdered her after she left him. Queen Nazli was deprived of her title and her money. She is rumoured to have become a Roman Catholic, confirmed by Bulent whom I met much later in Geneva. When he and Faiza went to visit her in California, the only gift the Queen gave her daughter was a Bible. For the mother of an important Moslem monarch to become a Christian was a great humiliation for him, apart from the rest of her behaviour.

And he did not get on with the princes and nabils of the Royal Family. This was not new. When the Khedive Ismaïl received the right of primogeniture from the Sultan, the next in line to the throne in the old system, Princes Fazil and Halim began plotting his downfall. The first was his younger brother and the second his uncle. There was no question of plotting when Farouk became king. There was a faction who believed that Prince Abdel Moneim, son of the Khedive Abbas Helmi II deposed by the British, had a right to the throne. The older princes were critical of the young king and disapproved of his life style, but made no effort to give him backing or affection. In fact, the Crown Prince, Prince Mohamed Ali Tewfik, was certain that Lampson would depose Farouk and give him the throne. He was openly critical and instead of helping the young King in the midst of vast political complications, he jeered at him and became great friends with Sir Miles. To give the King advice of any sort was, of course, a very delicate matter because he was touchy, had an inferiority complex and disliked being opposed. I cannot think of one of the autocratic princes who would have had the patience or the will to help the King. My father tried, but soon gave up. The only man of any distinction in his immediate circle was Hassanein Pasha and when he was killed in a suspicious car accident on Kasr el Nil bridge, the King was left with nobody while the crises continued. We all knew Pulli Bey and the other Italians who surrounded the King and they were very nice men, but useless as far as good advice and political acumen were concerned, in fact they would not dare. The politicians were probably the ones who turned the King into a cynic. Also the hangers-on, who would do whatever he wanted, except anything of a dangerous nature. Some years later, Nasser came to the same conclusion.

After his divorce and the disaster in Palestine, he sank lower every day, not even pretending to act as a decent leader. His European honeymoon with Nariman, squandering money on a huge retinue and gambling for enormous stakes was carefully fed back to the people of Egypt. His enemies were growing: the Moslem Brotherhood, the Communists, some of the press and ultimately the Free Officers. But the King seemed just to wait for the end, although he did once again demand that the British leave the Suez Canal, and had Crown domains distributed to landless fellahin. He even managed to get rid of the hated Wafd after the burning of Cairo, however, that only hastened the end. Too little and much too late!

In February 1952, under Ali Maher, universities reopened. The government declared willingness for a larger cooperation with the US in exchange for technical assistance. Plans were announced for irrigation work in the delta. Negotiations resumed in Cairo between Great Britain and Egypt on the Suez Canal and the Sudan. But Ali Maher refused to dissolve Parliament and resigned. The King named Neguib el Hilali to succeed him, dissolved Parliament and announced new elections on May 18, but the Wafd called on all Egyptians to oppose the postponement of general elections. The Egyptian Ambassador returned to London.

Hilali is followed by Hussein Sirry and Hilali again, with Princess Fawzia's husband, Ismaïl Cherine as Minister of War. Then the King appoints Mortada el Maraghi, who was known as an honest man, but nobody could find him.

So the King let everything go. He did nothing, although warned several times well ahead of the actual coup. He was completely dominated by a feeling of fatalism, probably accentuated by his growing health problems. He was far too fat, and his life style was extremely bad for him. I know from the Head Nurse at the Clinique Cécil in Lausanne, where he had been for a check-up shortly before his death, that his doctors had told him if he did not lose weight, he was going to die. His heart could not stand the strain much longer. Perhaps the boast that he was murdered by one of Nasser's henchmen was only that, a boast. On the other hand, Nasser was obsessed by the King, terrified that somehow he might regain his throne. In Egypt, the slightest rumour in connection with a royalist revival was treated with the utmost severity. The rare Egyptians who managed to travel were scared stiff of meeting with the King, because once back home, they would be grilled by the Secret Service and possibly even jailed.

He knew about the planned military coup, even the names of the Free Officers. Daddy went to see him at Ras el Tin Palace, begging him not to sign the abdication paper, saying he'd bring the Labour Party into the streets. The Navy and the Royal Guard were also faithful to the King. But he refused, although it was rumoured that he had contacted both the Americans and the British, requesting their help. None was forthcoming. The Americans were in favour of the Free Officers, having written off Farouk as a loser. Their handling of foreign policy is generally catastrophic, especially for the country in question. They also hate royalty. Their obsession with so-called democracy is infantile, insisting that people who can neither read nor write should vote, with no political parties and therefore no alternatives to their present rulers.

This was not the case in Egypt I hasten to add, but the alternative to the King which we finally got, ruined the country financially and put it back fifty years at least. Egypt's entire elite emigrated, together with most foreigners and the country was left with the totally unschooled. As for corruption, no comment. Both the US and Great Britain would rue the day they chose the Free Officers.

The ex-King spent the next thirteen years of his exile between Italy and Switzerland. He had installed his children near Lausanne, but he lived in Rome. The scandal press occasionally wrote about him and his girl friends, but generally he was left alone. I've often wondered how he must have judged the world that had so implacably judged him. On one occasion, he mentioned that the people to whom he had been kindest and most generous were the first to turn against him. We saw just that in Egypt after the revolution. Sometimes, we had marvellous surprises: people from whom we expected nothing, mostly people we did not know too well, would appear to help or befriend us. But, even before the revolution, the King had seen treachery from many quarters, and if he often behaved very badly, there were times when you could find excuses for him.

I cannot remember when I saw the King last. Probably in a nightclub. There were fewer invitations to the Palace. I think they declined when he divorced Queen Farida. At first, Princesses Fawzia and Faïza received, and later Queen Nariman. I had only two marvelous years in Egypt after returning from America, and then there was the revolution. I think what angers us most is how such a promising boy could ruin everything not only for himself and his immediate family, but for the rest of us and for the people of Egypt.

After the excesses of Nasser, meeting with some Egyptians in Europe, he asked them laughingly if Egypt had not been more agreeable under him. "You know, it is not easy to rule Egypt," he said.

I was in Rome when he died, on my way to Salerno to see my sister, who was to give birth any day to her first child. I went to the King's apartment in Parioli to pay a visit of condolence to his children. I found a shrine to Egypt. Nothing of value, but all Egyptian. The King's three daughters and his son, ex-Queen Farida, his first cousin Nazli Sabry, her husband Omar Cherine, who had been a chamberlain at the Palace, Prince Amr Ibrahim, Ibrahim Momtaz, a cousin of Queen Farida's, and Saïd Chaarawi, a great admirer of the King, and I attended the so-called funeral. The preceding day, his children and I had covered the casket with the former Egyptian flag, a crescent with three stars on a green background. We walked from the morgue to a special room at the cemetery which could be used until we found out where he was to be buried. Queen Farida phoned Cairo and threatened to have him buried in Saudi Arabia if Nasser refused to let him be buried in Egypt. Finally, he was buried at night in the Cherine lot. Later, under Sadat, he was buried in the Rifai mosque where all rulers are normally buried.

* * *

Ulvia married Shehriar Ratib on February 7th, 1952 and I married Salah el Orabi on August 12th of the same year. Neither of our husbands were members of the Royal Family which was a godsend.

Ulvia and Shehriar were married in Saïd Toussoun's house in Zamalek, as Garden City was no longer ours and our apartment in Maspero was not up to such a wedding. The King of England had just died and our Court was in mourning. The Palace agreed to the ceremony taking place, provided there was no music or dancing. We had a tea and the newly-weds drove off to Alexandria for their honeymoon.

After the revolution, we still danced on the edge. Parties, the Guezira Club, but not the Auto. Dad was no longer president of anything, and lived in our house in Schutz when he was not in prison. He had a little money left and managed for a while.

We were not yet social pariahs in 1952. Daddy was as outspoken as ever, and kept in or out of jail, was fast becoming one. The people who licked his boots a few months before were now pretending not to see him in public. He soon realised that the new government was worse than the old one, and began saying what he thought of the Free Officers. This earned him house arrest; then he was jailed with ex-ministers and prime ministers, members of the Wafd party, rich men, Communists, Moslem Brothers, etc.

An American journalist asked General Mohamed Naguib, the new President of the Republic, if his regime did not feel stable enough to release political prisoners like Abbas Halim. It would seem my mother had exerted pressure in Washington.

"But Abbas is a troublemaker," Naguib sighed. "For a year, since he's been in jail, we have had no strikes. When Abbas is out, we have strikes."

In 1953, he stood before the "Revolution Tribunal." The charge was treason. Dad refused an attorney. In the courtroom before the session, the press asked him what he thought the verdict would be. The hangman or freedom, he replied with a smile. In his testimony, he scorned Fouad, ridiculed Farouk, and most of all, blasted Nazli. Abbas Halim spoke his mind.

He was given a 15-year suspended sentence. Members of the tribunal were Abdel Latif el Boghdadi, Anwar el Sadat and Hassan Ibrahim. Boghdadi told the press the suspended sentence would hang over Abbas Halim's head in case he thought of fomenting trouble again.

Later, he was sent to El Tor, a very nasty place on the Red Sea, normally inhabited by hardened criminals. Daddy organised his life there: he had a toilet cleaned and disinfected by a group of detainees who guarded the loo as his private property. He was on good terms with everybody, except the guards.

Ulvia and Shehriar Rateb's wedding, Zamalek, 1952

This to the great joy of the criminals. When we finally got him out, the grief of these men was something to see. He shared the cigarettes and any other goodies we managed to send him with his new friends and they adored him.

After the revolution, Dad's life was over. It was tragic but he refused to be affected. He was soon quite penniless, had no freedom really, most of his old friends were either in the same boat or avoided him. The new rulers soon undid most of the sports organisations he had set up or they went to pot because of neglect. He was allowed to live rent-free in the Schutz house, but it had been confiscated and everything in it was the property of the government. Later he managed with the connivance of the increasingly corrupt officials to sell some of the furniture. At the beginning he had refused a government pension, but he was to regret this futile gesture. None of us realised just how bad things were going to be.

***

I was flirting with both Salah and Shehriar's elder brother, Bourhan. Bulent decided that one Ratib was enough in the family, so after Salah made a fuss about this two-timing, I agreed to marry him. Ismaïl came out of hiding, probably feeling safe. If I could have made up with him, I'd have dropped everybody else.

Salah and I were married at another tea/garden party in Schutz. My witnesses were Bulent and Hassan Hassan. Mummy came over for my wedding, bringing my silver, crystal and china inherited from my Great Aunt Nazli Halim, but cleverly left it on board the ship and took it back with her. Our honeymoon was spent at the San Stefano Hotel, a forbidding stone structure with horrible furniture and absolutely nothing to recommend it, except for a lovely garden. And it was near Schutz. We spent most of our time

Prince Abbas Halim in prison, 1953

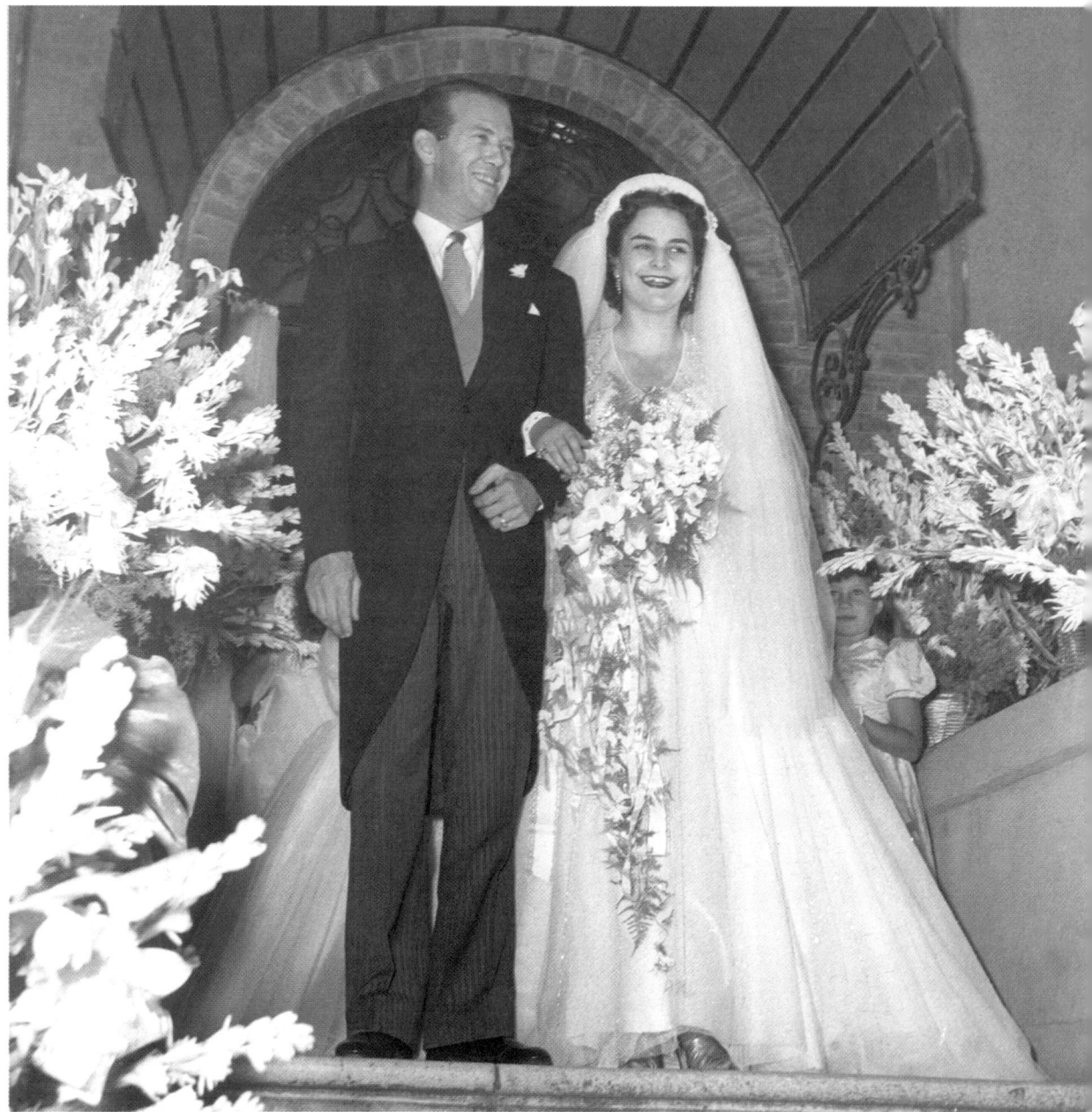

Nevine and Salah el Orabi, Schutz, 1952

at the beach, where Salah played backgammon non-stop with the other boys, while I sunbathed and swam. Not very romantic. Dad was put into house arrest soon after our wedding, so it was really not the time to be seen living it up in nightclubs. We visited Dad and occasionally went to the movies.

When the summer was over, we returned to Cairo. I had found a taker for my apartment in Zamalek in my new sister-in-law, Fawkia. She was a darling and I loved her very much. Salah insisted on continuing to live in Maadi and made such a fuss that I agreed. It was a big mistake, because we had to spend an enormous amount of time driving to and from Maadi. Nobody wanted to come to Maadi for dinner and even less for lunch. Salah had the most marvellous cook and every time I think of how little we used him, I could burst into tears. We did lunch at home most days and Salah got me to lose 10 kgs thanks to the cook's way with grilled meat and salads.

We went out every night, mostly to the roof of the Semiramis in summer and the Grill in winter. The roof was one of those places that people remember for the rest of their lives. It was not particularly luxurious, just a large terrace on two levels with the bar a few steps down ahead as you came in and the dance floor with tables around it on your right. The band, led by Bob Azzam with Jimmy, a very popular singer, was excellent. Bob Azzam opened a cabaret in Geneva after the revolution and became very well-known. The Semiramis was on the Nile, with only a narrow road between the hotel and the river. After a hot day, it was such a relief to breathe cooler air from the desert in the evening. Cairo was much less polluted then, fewer people, fewer cars. At other times, we went to the Mena House near the Pyramids, where there was another terrace. It gave on the gardens of the hotel, which were very lovely, with the Pyramids as a backdrop. There was an Italian singer with the band, called Sandro, who was all the rage.

At that time, our great friend, James Murray, told a friend of ours that he thought the Royal Family had behaved with great dignity. I don't see what else we could have done. Pulling out our hair would not have made matters any better. We were, however, still at the beginning of our trials.

Daddy had remarried in secret, just after the revolution. The lady was a cousin of Mummy's, Nafia Yeghen. Her first husband had been a Turkish imperial prince, Orhan Effendi, from whom she had a daughter called Nedjla. Daddy finally admitted it to us, but not to Granny. She came to visit him one day, and Stepmama rushed to kiss her hand. Granny asked her who she was, she said: "I'm Abbas' wife." "Nonsense," said Granny and called Daddy to confirm this. Daddy sheepishly admitted the truth and Granny immediately left the house in a fury. It took years for her to forgive him. Typical male cowardice.

Life continued. We still went to Zohria, but Faiza was trying to get out of Egypt. She and Bulent still had us, the core group, always ready to help. Salah Salem, one of the Free Officers, was introduced to Faiza and fell in love with her. Thanks to him, she finally managed to leave, taking most of her jewels with her. Her and Bulent's idea of money management was quite catastrophic and they went through most of what they had at a rapid pace. Then they divorced and Faiza ended in California, having refused umpteen offers of very advantageous marriages in Europe. I saw her twice before she left for the States, once in Paris at a party and once in Geneva when she called me to go meet her there. She was in fine form and looked great. I saw Bulent only once, in a Geneva nightclub. He was full of optimism, saying life was unexpected and wonderful. Salah was with him that evening, but we did not speak. Bulent did many funny things, like becoming a sufi guru. He even married again, and after a few hard times, it seemed he was doing well when he died of heart failure. Faiza remained in Los Angeles, where she died of cancer in 1993.

It took one year for the Free Officers to decide that the Royal Family was an unnecessary headache. They abolished the monarchy and proclaimed a

*Victor Bersolesi, Prince Abbas Halim, Nafia Yeghen, Farouk Effendi
and Nedjla Orhan, Schutz*

republic. At the same time they took away all our possessions. We were allowed one house to live in, one car per family, no land, buildings, jewels, money in any form. We were responsible for keeping the house and everything in it in good condition. We could not sell anything. Salah quickly proved he was not a member of the Mohamed Ali family and never put money in the bank, he had it all at home. Shehriar, however, had serious financial problems and it was months before he could organise himself. He could not even pay the rent. His landlady, Madame Lakah, was very understanding and told him to pay when he could. Many of our other cousins were in a similar situation. And some of the princes, among whom were Ismaïl and Hassan Hassan, had absolutely nothing. They were finally given a pension, Hassan got £E 28 and Ismaïl because he'd been in the Air Force during the war with Israel, received considerably more, I think £E 75.

The new rulers began to throw their weight around. They had no idea how to govern a country, scarcely surprising, and mistrusted all members of the *ancien régime*. At first, they may have had an honest desire to give all classes a chance in life. They began with limiting the amount of land one person could own. After the confiscation of the Royal Family, now alluded to as the "Family of Mohamed Ali", they sequestered rich Egyptians and nationalised both Egyptian and foreign industries. Most foreigners left as no compensation was forthcoming or was offered in the guise of worthless bonds.

Nasser's takeover of the Suez Canal and the fiasco of the 1956 war *won* by Egypt (thanks to Eisenhower forcing Britain, France and Israel to withdraw) made Nasser more popular in Egypt and the Arab countries. He called it the "Triple and Cowardly Aggression." He was a past master in the art of propaganda and got out of the worst situations with brio.

And all the while the government was rapidly ruining Egypt. They also had to deal with a large number of people who were profiting from the chaos to settle old scores. In Nasser's book, he complains bitterly about the avalanche of requests he received to punish enemies who had nothing to do with politics. Sadat says that if somebody was accused of insulting him or a member of his family, Nasser would not even bother to check the truth of the story before lowering the boom. The atmosphere became more and more stifling. People were put in jail just for criticising the Army, viz. my father. Travel was forbidden, except for extreme and proven health reasons or if you were over 65. The amount of money you could take out was limited. The phones were tapped and some people were followed by car. One instance when Salah and I were driving home together for a change, we were followed quite openly by another car. Salah had just bought a small Fiat and we wondered how they knew it was him. He spent money so he was suspect.

The "purity", "honesty" and "self-sacrifice" of the new lot was fast disappearing. Most of the Crown jewels, as well as the personal jewels of the Royal Family, furniture, antiques, painting, etc. which happened to catch the eye of an important member of the junta never showed up at the auctions which were subsequently held. In Alexandria today, there is a museum which pretends to display the jewels belonging to the Mohamed Ali family. There is nothing much in that *museum*. The really good pieces were stolen at the time of the revolution. I know for a fact that one officer's wife showed up at a prestigious French jeweller's trying to sell a necklace belonging to a member of the Royal Family. In the jeweller's books, this person had absolutely no right to sell this piece of jewellery. Had the Egyptian government tried to sell it, that would have been different as confiscation was accepted as a fact of life, whereas stealing was not—yet.

***

Married life was quite nice to begin with. Salah and I got on quite well and there were no subjects of discord. After the summer, we returned to Cairo. Living in Maadi was a real pain, but I was a good sport. In the morning, Salah often went to the Maadi Sporting Club to play tennis. We lunched together and then he'd go to the Guezira Sporting Club, where I joined him. I was horribly bored sitting for hours on the Lido doing nothing or talking to the same people about the same things for the umpteenth time.

I began taking piano lessons at the Tiegerman Conservatory in town. I did not qualify to being taught by the Maestro himself, but had a lovely lady, Madame Marianos, who took me on. I worked harder than at AUC, but cannot pretend to being passionately dedicated to the piano. I could play very nicely at times, but I realised my limitations early on. It was doing something worthwhile even if I was not bringing marvellous music to the world. I always had difficulty reading music and hated solfège. Not only did you have to read the notes, but also the tempo and that was my downfall. I did not have a particularly good ear either. But I persisted and even have a photo of myself playing at Ewart Memorial Hall in one of the student concerts given by the Conservatory. I played Liszt's Third Consolation and trembled all over, including my leg on the pedal. A recording was made of all participants and I sound like Rubinstein.

Otherwise, we continued in the usual way. Daddy was imprisoned twice more, and then finally they left him in peace. He had no apartment in Cairo now and generally stayed at Ulvia's or at the Lotus Hotel, managed by an old friend of his, Georges Zalzal. He came out with us in Cairo and also saw his old pals, Paul and Laky Zervudachi, the best friends anyone could have.

266

Aswan 1956

At Ewart Memorial Hall, AUC, Cairo, April 14, 1954

The marriage continued well, until the husband of one of my best friends, pointed out to me that his wife and my husband seemed to dance an awful lot together. I could not have been more surprised, but once suspicion and jealousy raise their ugly heads, beware! And there went the marriage! To this day, I have no idea why that brute made that remark. A brute who beat his wife when in his cups. The frequency depended on his finances and as they were mostly precarious, he thought he had found the ideal solution in Salah who always paid the bill unless we were specifically invited.

I became jealous of every female in sight, and seeing this, Salah pretended to flirt with anything in a skirt. I reciprocated. Too many good-looking men and beautiful women, alcohol, parties, dancing, all that is required to ruin a marriage.

Salah, quite sadistic at times, could remain for days without speaking to me. I could not stand that and it was always I who begged to be forgiven, even if not guilty. Supposedly, before we married, he was mad about me, called me his goddess. I knew he thought that I was still in love with Ismail and at first he was right. But I soon began to fall in love with him. Horrendous mistake.

He might not have been very bright, but people have a sixth sense about such situations. He decided to get his own back, at me and at the brute, who had seduced his first wife. I became the most boring of creatures, all other women were preferable to me. He never sat next to me except when forced to by circumstances, never talked to me in public, never gave a mark of affection. He generally ignored me.

I could never find out when Salah and his supposed girlfriend met. They both sat on the terrace of the Sporting Club all afternoon in full sight of everybody. Their absences at the same time were rare and generally explained at once. But I was sure something was going on because Salah wanted revenge on the husband of this woman. Once I overheard two of my men friends saying

269

not to let me know; one of them was Ismaïl. It was his fault that I was now married to this sadist.

In the meantime, I played the housewife. I brought some of the furniture from my Zamalek flat and redid the curtains, removed the ghastly ornaments and replaced them with silver ashtrays, cigarette boxes, crystal vases and books. I was in charge of paying for the food, and discussing menus with the cook if necessary. Salah was in charge of extras, like booze. My talent as an interior decorator took another beating: I placed the new curtains in the living room too high up and Bulent ordered me to have them lowered at once. Salah was very nice about it.

Salah had a bull mastiff called Duke, who took a dim view of me and it was a long time before he accepted me and before I conquered my fear of him. I had to leave my chow, Toffee, in Alex. Finally, when I caught German measles and was in quarantine for three weeks, Duke and I went for walks around Maadi. Salah did not bother much with me, but continued his usual routine. I remonstrated once, saying if you were married, you should take the bad with the good and he might stay with me once in a while. He did not even vouchsafe a reply. It's true that when he fell ill with a bad case of flu, he insisted I go out and carry on as usual. He did allow me to change his pyjamas when he was soaked with perspiration and, miraculously, was even grateful. This good "entente" did not last very long. Salah and I had absolutely nothing in common. His education was minimal and he never read a book. Music and art did not interest him, and I can't remember him ever setting foot in a museum. Anyone who can sit five to six hours in a chair doing nothing and barely speaking, must have something missing. He did play chess once in a while and was not too bad at it, denoting some brain activity.

This state of affairs continued for about four years. Once in a while, there was a huge row, then things calmed down, mostly thanks to me. We met a charming Indian diplomat at a party and as Salah was playing his usual game, I decided to give him the lesson of his life. I flirted furiously with the Indian, went to the Auberge in his convertible and danced the night away with him. This time, Salah reacted. He was furious, complaining to my cousin Nimet's husband, Mounir. He wanted a divorce, etc. etc. and, of course, he sulked. In the end, we patched it up. This feeling of insecurity was very bad for the marriage; at the least problem, he or I immediately talked of divorce. I did try to give the marriage a chance, did not want a divorce at all, but both partners have to work and Salah was certainly not. Sometimes I wondered why he married me at all. I was wife No. 3. Before he married Tata, wife No. 2, he'd had a terrific row with her and gone off and married a poor girl on the rebound. When he made up with Tata, he divorced wife No. 1 with no compunction and eloped with Tata. They were ostracised by her family and most of their friends. Then they lost their little son and the marriage broke up. Salah, heartbroken, went off to Europe to pull himself together. When I moved into his house in Maadi, I found the child's room untouched since his death. I threw everything out and refurnished it as a guest room. I even got Salah to enter the room and inspect it. I'd done a good job and he no longer shunned the room.

He did one positive thing for me: he made me lose 10 kg and I never looked better. As proof, I have clippings from the Society pages of various newspapers and lots of photos. Mum sent me a friend of hers, Roberta Regan, and we took her out with Ismaïl as her escort. In the photos, he does not look very happy, but I look complacent and indifferent to everybody.

Another time, the First Secretary of the Iranian Embassy, came up to me at the Guezira Club to ask if I had Princess Fawzia's phone number, because Princess Shams, the Shah's sister was in town and wanted to speak to her. I got it for him through Nazli Sabry Cherine. To thank me, Salah and I were invited to the Auberge with the Princess, her husband, her lady-in-waiting and the First Secretary. It seems that the Shah had sent a message to Fawzia, asking her if he could help her in any way. A beautiful gesture. Salah behaved very well on this extremely boring occasion. He was a closet snob.

At a cocktail party, I found him chatting up a very pretty woman, the wife of a French diplomat, and organising a game of tennis with her. I promptly said I'd join them and proposed a partner to make up a doubles. Salah did not mind at all, but the lady was no longer interested. Was I learning at last? Not really. I still got carried away and went too far.

At one point, he went off to Europe on business alone. He informed me in front of Daddy one evening at the Semiramis that he'd taken Irene Pappas out to dinner. Somehow the conversation turned to asking him if he'd been to bed with her. I immediately informed him that if he had I'd divorce him at once. Then I accused poor Dad of being a very bad husband when married to Mum. Perfectly true, but Dad was furious with me. I was full of tact!

We went off to Ras el Bar with Fawkia, Ismaïl and an air force friend of his. The houses, made of straw, are called *eishas* and are very attractive. We, however, ended in a filthy hotel made of stone. In the evening we met Abdel Latif Boghdadi, one of the Free Officers, and a friend of Ismaïl's from his air force days. We all went to the Girbi on the river and smoked hashish. I was too frightened to inhale and it was a complete fiasco for me. It did not affect the others much either. That was the last hash party for me.

There were still lots of parties. We were friends with the Turkish Ambassador, a charming bachelor, a perfect gentleman with intelligence and humour. We were invited to the Embassy both on official occasions as well as in small groups. The French Ambassador, Couve de Murville, also invited us. France did not think much of the new crowd and our invitation card read: "Princess Nevine Halim and Mr. Salah el Orabi." Hadidja Hassan told me that one dinner at the French Embassy, Princess Isabelle, daughter of the Comte de Paris, had been guest of honour and had been treated as if France was still a kingdom.

Other favourite diplomats were Mr. Almagro, the Cuban Minister (before Castro), who gave delightful parties and often joined us at the Auberge or Semiramis and the Dutch Ambassador and Mrs. Knoop Coopmans, who gave marvellous balls in the garden of the Embassy. The Embassy was opposite the Toussoun house, which had been confiscated.

The outings when the "girlfriend" was not with us, generally went well and Salah seemed another person. It was not only the "girlfriend" who spoiled the evening but also the husband. He was a drunk and often became abusive and disagreeable, which made the atmosphere heavy with foreboding. There is nothing more boring than a drunk. First, to keep him happy, you have to listen to him repeating the same thing over and over. Then you must agree with everything he says.

Fawkia joined us occasionally. She had two daughters from her first marriage to Kamel Wassef who were lovely girls. Now divorced, she was besieged by at least three suitors. I'm sorry to say that she chose the wrong one. Ibrahim Khalil was a Turk and a pain. He could be charming at times, but normally he was obstinate, small-minded and tactless. Salah disliked him on sight. Fawkia produced a son, Tarek, and then the marriage began to sputter. They left for Libya, where Ibrahim had a job. He was an architect and apparently a good one. Fawkia hated Libya, especially Tripoli where they lived. She returned to Egypt when Salah died and sent her son to be educated at an American school in Greece. Her financial situation was bad, and Ibrahim refusing to cooperate in this plan, she began to make costume jewellery, which I sold for her in Lausanne. She managed and had nothing more to do with her husband.

Salah was a curious man. He visited his mother, who adored him, about once a year. Taking me to meet her before our marriage was a great concession. She was an undemanding and kind person. She'd been married several times, and I think Salah disapproved of this. His father had died when he was quite young and he inherited a large fortune. He treated his sisters much the same as his mother, except that he saw a lot of Fawkia who frequented the same people as he did. She was his twin and I think his favourite. Leila, who was older, had been an excellent pianist. Her husband, Ihab Almaz, died in the same plane crash as Aunt Emina Fazil, supposedly carrying the Crown jewels of Italy out of the country. Leila was another strange creature. Hugely generous, she ended up without a cent thanks to an adopted nasty, ungrateful girl who stole everything when she grew up. She even sold Leila's phone.

Salah was very proud of Khourshid Pasha, one of his ancestors on his mother's side, also known as "Parmaksiz" (minus a finger in Turkish) because he lost a finger fighting the Wahabites in Arabia under Ibrahim Pasha. To be of Turkish descent was a mark of distinction at that time.

***

I had developed breathlessness and fatigue after all the parties, marital squabbles and political upheavals. After a check-up at Dr. Mohamed Ibrahim's, a renowned heart specialist, he informed me that my heart was in bad shape and that I must have an operation unless I wanted to die of asphyxiation. He was very insistent that I have the operation as soon as possible. Also, as he'd heard I was recently married, I must on no account have a baby. The strain on the heart would be too much for me.

This was not exactly good news but it was the best way to obtain an exit visa and money as the operation could not be performed in Egypt.

*Salah, Sonya Assem, Fawkia el Orabi, Prince Hassan Hassan and Nevine
at the Semiramis Roof*

As I could not travel alone, my husband had to come with me. We obtained a list of all the best heart specialists in Europe, and with a sense of deliverance, embarked on the *Marseillaise*, a French ship of the Messageries Maritimes Line. We had a luxurious cabin suite, with a balcony overlooking the sea. The ship was not huge but well fitted, the food was good and the wines French!

That year, Salah had given me a new car, as my red Buick Roadmaster convertible given to me by Dad was starting to show its age. It had been confiscated and would eventually revert to the government. The Royal Family had low number plates and mine was Cairo 70. Before the revolution, policemen saluted us. I find that difficult to believe now.

I gave Ali the Buick to finish off and took my new Chevrolet to Europe with us as we intended to drive around France, Italy and Switzerland.

We landed in Marseilles and drove to Geneva, via great eating places, such as Valence, Vienne and Lyon. Geneva is where the money was, of course. I also visited my great-aunt Bedia, our beloved Auntie Tabby, Granny's sister. She lived in Lausanne at the Hotel Alexandra and travelled around Europe, mostly to Germany. She had very bad asthma and could not stand the heat and dust of Egypt. We stayed at the Hôtel du Rhône in Geneva and met up with some friends. We were soon off again and drove to Paris stopping at more great eating places on the way: Dijon, Saulieu, Avallon, Auxerre, and finally Paris.

We stayed at the Prince de Galles, a prestigious hotel on Avenue George V, next to the George V Hotel. My great friend, Nanou, now Princess Saïd Toussoun, was still in Paris. She invited me to lunch and another time took me to the races in Longchamps. She picked me up at the hotel in her Rolls and as I climbed into the car, Dean Martin walking by, stopped to admire us. He was pretty gorgeous himself.

We had quite a lot of friends either living in Paris, or passing through. Hassan Momtaz had a flat in Paris and invited us to a cocktail party there. His wife, my cousin Adleya, had not yet arrived from Egypt and the guests were a rather strange lot. Salah and I left after a couple of drinks.

We also played the tourists, going to the Monseigneur, a beautiful Russian cabaret. Gypsy music was played to us as we sipped our champagne. I loved it! On to the Eléphant blanc and Madame Artur where transvestites performed. You would never have guessed that these beautiful women were really men. At the Thèâtre des Dix Heures, we laughed at wonderful French wit. We had drinks at the bar of the Plaza Athénée and at the Ritz, the most luxurious hotels in Paris.

From there, we went to Turin, where I saw a heart specialist who said that since I was going to the United States, there was no point having tests here too. We stayed at the Principe de Piemonte, where our room was like a hangar and the bathroom not much smaller. We dined at a restaurant outside town, on a terrace with vines covering the trellis over our heads, a stream trickling below and greenery everywhere.

We took the Via Aurelia to Rome. Salah loved Italy, especially Rome. It was sensational at that time and wildly popular as a location for film making. Rosselini had just produced his best films, and world famous American movie stars were strolling down Via Veneto and sitting at the bar of the Excelsior Hotel. We met Lex Barker, who had just divorced from Lana Turner because she wanted him to beat her up while they made love and he just could not. Also saw Joan Crawford, who had the reputation of being a first class bitch. Linda Christian was at the Excelsior too, and the lift operator told my husband that it was a pity he had his wife with him, because great things were going on in Miss Christian's apartment. Tyrone Power had died recently, and Linda had the care of their two daughters, but that did not put a brake on her activities. I saw Ava Gardner several times, once close up as she entered a room at the hotel. She was wearing a green satin dress and this brought out the green of her eyes and she looked exactly like a panther. One of the most beautiful women I have ever seen. She was flirting with Walter Chiari then and we saw them several more times in various trattorias.

In Rome, we had even more friends than in Paris. There was Rick de Portanova, an old pal of Salah's, a darling and wonderfully handsome. He was to become extremely rich later on, inheriting oil fields in Texas through his mother's family, but at the moment, he was very badly off. He was married to a lovely Swedish ex-model called Ingrid. Then there was Moritz de Hesse, who had managed to get some of his mother's property back and had a lovely house in Villa Savoia. Our friend, Piffo, was in Rome as well as Stefan Boideff who had married a Russian, Tatiana, once Christian Dior's star model.

At the Excelsior, I broke my arm racing Salah to the bathroom in our room and slipped on the parquet. After a very bad night, we went to the general hospital, where they told me nothing was wrong.

We met Stefan and Tatiana for lunch and they immediately took us to a clinic. They told us the general hospital was useless, like our Kasr El Aini. So I had a proper X-ray and found I'd broken my left arm, but the bone was not out of place. My arm was put in a stiff bandage but not in a cast.

From Rome, we drove to Cannes along the superb Italian Riviera via Portofino, Santa Margarita Ligure, Rapallo. We spent a night in Portofino, had drinks and dinner on a floating bar anchored in the harbour. In Cannes we stayed at the Hotel Martinez, where we joined up with Hassan. Unfortunately, he was with his girlfriend and when his wife rang from Paris and a woman answered from his bedroom, she would have nothing more to do with him, and they ended by divorcing. He married the girlfriend.

Salah and I drove to St. Tropez which was already becoming a favourite summer resort of the jet set. We could not find a room anywhere. At one point we were blocking a very narrow street outside the Hotel Ail au Lit, and with

Moritz de Hesse, Tania, Nevine, Stefan, Ibrahim Khalil and Salah in Rome

our Egyptian number plates and the fact that Nasser had just nationalised the Suez Canal, the French started to make jokes: "blocking the Suez Canal is not enough, you have to come to St. Tropez and block our streets too." Salah had the Arabic part of the number plates covered in black paint, just in case things got worse. We went to Tahiti beach with Fayed Sabit where nudists were supposed to gather, but only saw a man presumably naked behind a bush. With Fayed, we also went to the La Bonne Auberge at Antibes for a memorable lunch. Again with Fayed, we had a big scare. It was in Juan Les Pins, and I had rushed across the street because I'd seen a bottle of Arpège, my perfume, at a sensational price in a shop window. When I rejoined the boys, I slipped on the steps leading to the bar we were going to and fell on the same arm. I still had a bandage on it and the bar owner noticed and immediately produced a Cognac for me. I never got near the Cognac, because Salah drank it down in one go. Mercifully, I felt nothing and later in Cannes we had an X-ray done, but apart from breaking a little more, it did not hurt at all and I was soon able to get rid of the bandage.

Back to Rome via Florence, where we spent the night at one of the CIGA hotels, another Excelsior. We walked through the streets of Florence in the evening and later drove up into the hills whence we had a spectacular view of the magnificent city.

The autostradas barely existed and I remember the ghastly curves Salah had to negotiate between Florence and Rome on the Via Flaminia. He did not let me drive, and poor Salah had a tough time.

We went to a few more great places which either no longer exist or have deteriorated badly. The Osteria del Orso was beautiful: it was on three floors, the first being the bar, the second the restaurant and the third the nightclub. It was an authentic old house which had been lovingly restored and adapted to its new function. There was Giorgio's, a bar and restaurant just behind the

Excelsior. George was alive then and received all his "guests" himself. At Trastevere, our favourite was La Cisterna, with good food and lots of music and singing. La Taverna Flavia was a favourite among movie stars and the jet set. The owner when informed that Ulvia and I were Egyptian princesses looked us up in the Almanach de Gotha. One of our friends chastised him for being so suspicious and the poor man answered that every third person who entered his restaurant claimed to have a title. This time he decided to check.

***

Salah and I had another few weeks in Rome before I flew to the States to see the heart specialist. He was returning to Cairo until we found out if I was to be operated on or not. This exile lasted for nearly a year. Ulvia came to join me when I had to undergo tests, supposedly to comfort Mummy, but mostly to get out of Egypt. Ali was in Washington working in a store selling electrical supplies.

Mum's friends were all high placed government and military people, like Omar Bradley, millionaire party givers like Gwen Cafritz and Perle Mesta and diplomats galore, like Maurice Couve de Murville, the charming French Ambassador, and Aba Eban, the Israeli Ambassador whose wife had grown up in Egypt and had lived opposite us in Zamalek.

We made a clique of our own, some issuing from Mummy's friends, but most of them we met on our own. The Egyptian Ambassador was Ahmed Hussein who had married Leila Shoukry, the grad student I'd met at Bryn Mawr. In spite of the revolution, they were very nice to us. We were really hated by Egyptians after the revolution thanks to that envious, horrible Nasser who blamed us for every ill. Nasser even erased the Mohamed Ali era from school history books.

These days, with the word corruption taking on new dimensions, the "bad old days" are seen in a different light. They seem almost ridiculous compared with what goes on today. Mohamed Ali Pasha and Ibrahim Pasha, his warrior son, are named with pride, and King Fouad and King Farouk's effigies appear on key rings and silver ashtrays. The "Egyptianisation" of the country has ruined it, and the "Arabisation" has finished the job. "Egypt for the Egyptians" has produced one of the most corrupt countries in the world, which runs somehow against every probability, literally on a prayer.

We return to Washington D.C. in the fall of 1956. After a few months at the Mayflower, Ulvia and I rented a flat in Georgetown. The hotel was getting us down and was very expensive. We spent most of our time eating and managed to put on a lot of weight. I did not put on the famous 10 kg lost earlier, but we had to stop lying around doing nothing. At least with the flat we had to move, clean the place and eventually cook. The only thing I could cook was scrambled eggs, and I have no idea where I learned it.

Ali would come over to join us for food and drink or going out. Poor darling, he was pretty lonely and the Mater spent most of her time quarrelling with him. So he was delighted to have us to come to. He lived in the basement of Mummy's building at that time.

Poor Ali had a rough time after the revolution. He had refused to continue at Stanford Military Academy after our return to Egypt in 1950 and was living in Alexandria when Dad was confiscated. He had no money and survived by killing the chickens and ducks for food. Sometimes he came to stay with Ulvia and Shehriar or Salah and me in Cairo, but he disliked our lifestyle. At last, Mum arranged for him to fly to the Washington via Paris, but she was in a tiny room at the Mayflower and had no money to send him to school. He took odd jobs. He was allowed to live in a room on the ground floor of 2339 Mass, so at least he did not pay rent. Mummy drove him mad. When he had a job,

Nevine in Georgetown

Prince Mohamed Ali Abbas Halim

she complained he never came to see her, and when he didn't have work, she accused him of malingering.

He never got a degree. But he became Chief Engineer of the World Bank.

He says, "Im a mechanic." Dad once told him, "You were born a prince. Now you must learn to be a gentleman."

He is a prince and a gentleman, my little brother.

***

Mummy and Mr. Rediker were divorcing and she lived at the Mayflower again, in a very modest room. He had turned out to be a very bad bet. A fortune hunter and a thief. He stole lots of things from Mum's apartment. She rented the apartment as there was no money coming out of Egypt and she was being accused of fraudulently taking money out of the country. She had to make out with what she had in the States, which consisted mostly of the building on Massachusetts Avenue, her jewels and the paintings Daddy had bought for her. Our mother was much better with money than Daddy, but she was no financier. She sold the building subsequently, gave most of the money to her friend the jeweller, Mr. Albert Kramer, to invest for her. He gave her an excellent return on investment until he had a late-life crisis, went to the Côte d'Azur and gambled away all his and all Mummy's money. She had no proof, nothing signed and got a settlement from his daughters in the form of a tiny amount. It was good of them to even give her that much, because I believe they had to get it from their husbands, as "Papa" left them nothing.

Aunt Emina Toussoun also lived in Washington, having married Connie Bretsch, whom she had met in Cairo during the War. They lived in Georgetown and often invited us to Sunday dinner, which we especially liked as Auntie would cook a "mean hamburger" and we would stuff like little pigs. Mummy

285

was frightfully jealous of Aunt Emina and they spent a lot of time feuding and making up. It seems many people had warned Mummy about Rediker. I think she was more interested in getting back at Daddy than anything else. Auntie said that Frank and Mummy drank far too much and that Mum got rather pissed when she went out. Poor Mummy, things had turned out pretty badly for her. The beloved husband gone west, the daughters married and indifferent, or so she thought. She was extremely difficult in her old age.

Ulvia and I spent the winter months quite agreeably. A friend of ours, Bill Thompson, took Ulvia to dinner at the Kennedys, who also lived in Georgetown. Jack was only a senator then, but was already making a name for himself. He was supposedly going to arrange for her to attend a session of Congress, where Robert Kennedy was interrogating labour leaders, but he never got around to it. He did call to apologise. We also met Senator George Smathers, a friend of Jack Kennedy's, very handsome and very nice too. At the time he had a beautiful girlfriend called Julie. Ali still sees her at times, but she no longer lives in Washington.

Having a good time was one thing, but I'd come for a check-up. Thanks to our social life we met Dr. Amoroso, a cancer specialist, at a cocktail party given by Phyllis and Bob Lewis. Bill Amoroso, of Italian origin obviously, admired my Italian shoes and so we chatted a bit. We met him again a couple of times and finally on one occasion, I mentioned why I'd come to the United States. He immediately offered to help because one of his best friends was a heart surgeon, Dr. Charles Hufnagel. He arranged for me to be examined by Dr. Hufnagel at Georgetown University Hospital. Dr. Mohamed Ibrahim had been quite correct in advising an early operation; Dr. Hufnagel wanted to operate as soon as possible. After the various tests, he had found a much bigger hole in my heart than expected.

We had reached decision time. Mummy would not pronounce herself. Aunt

Emina said it was up to me, but she thought I ought to do it. So did I. Dr. Hufnagel was a pioneer in heart surgery and I trusted him completely. I was not afraid, probably because I was only 27 and quite unaware of the danger. I did understand the surgeon's concern, mostly thanks to Bill Amoroso, who was a surgeon himself and convinced me of the importance of my being in good condition rather than waiting for more expertise.

The next step was to advise Salah, get more money and set a date. We decided on April, before the summer heat. Salah arrived in New York and I went up to meet him, checking into the Sherry Netherlands hotel. I really liked that hotel, small but exclusive. The bar was especially appreciated, dark, but not too dark, with comfortable seats and sofas. We sat near a couple there one evening, began to talk and found them very congenial, so much so that they invited us to join them next day in what sounded uncommonly like an orgy. Salah's English was not very good and I was very naïve, but it did dawn on us eventually what we were getting into. We suddenly remembered another social engagement and excused ourselves.

After a few days in New York, we took the train to Washington. Salah seemed to like the flat, although the furniture was dreadful and we had done nothing much to pretty it up. It was certainly more "homey" than the hotel, and much cheaper in the long run. This is where our culinary inadequacies came to the fore, including Salah's. Out of ignorance and laziness, Salah heated up the same tea leaves in a metal pot every morning, only adding some water. Even Ulvia and I knew this was poisonous and persuaded him to brew a new pot every day. I don't know how he escaped a very severe stomach ache.

Before Salah's arrival, Ulvia and I had gone up to New York to meet Hassan Momtaz. We also found Victor Semeika with his new wife, Budge Patty, Jorge Sorrondo who'd been at the Argentine Embassy in Cairo and had since married Sybilla Szczeniowska, pronounced Chernovska. She had been Ali Khan's girlfriend and rumour had it that he'd fathered her son. Hassan produced some rich guys for us, but we did not like them much. One guy did slap my face after I refused to go to bed with him, although I'd led him on all evening. I richly deserved it and learned a much needed lesson. Here in tough New York, one could not lead men on as I did at home, where most of the time I knew them very well and they were all incredibly gentlemanly.

In Washington, we were nearing The Day. I was given a marvellous drug that made you feel you'd go to the guillotine with the greatest pleasure. I woke up towards the evening with the impression that I had an iron band around my chest. I was also in an oxygen tent, it was like a mosquito net. Mummy was having fits outside, but Auntie Emina came in to see me, and Uli and Ali had a peak. It seems the operation took much longer than expected as the hole was even bigger than the test showed. In fact, it was essential that I be operated on, because I would have died in a year or two from suffocation. The lungs would have been unable to purify the blood in time while the bad blood mixed with the good through the famous hole.

I did not really suffer that much, and when I did, the nurses gave me a hypo at once. The most disagreeable part was having to swallow a tube in order to get out all the blood and stuff in my lungs. That was really horrid. But I was made to get up on the third day in order to avoid blood clotting, and after that I recuperated very quickly. It was sensational and such a relief that it was over. Although I was considered to be very courageous, the idea of death did not occur to me before The Day. When one is young, it is not something you seriously consider. Now when I think of death, it is a serious option, in fact it has become inevitable.

After a fortnight, I was able to go home. It was extremely hot and humid by then and we only had air-conditioning in one room, where Ulvia and I had slept. Now that Salah had arrived, she very kindly gave him her bed and sweltered in the other very small bedroom. We tried to get her to come back with me, but she would not. Fortunately, the weather cooled and after one more check-up, we could sail to Europe.

Mummy, having played the Mater Dolorosa to the hilt, was getting sick of us and was delighted when we announced our departure. We planned to spend a few days in New York before sailing on the Augustus to Genoa. Ali came with us as did the Schniders, Di-di Lyon and Susan, a school friend of Ulvia's. We met up with Bob Widener in New York. Our last dinner was offered by the Schniders, but as the guest list grew, Fred's face got longer and longer. At the end of the evening, Salah realised that the invitation was going to be his. When you know how rich the Schniders were, it was quite unforgivable, especially as she talked about money non-stop.

Next day, Ali, Di-di, Susan and Bob came to the dock to see us off. I have a picture showing them waving to us and Ali looking so miserable. Poor darling, he'd been so happy with us there and a place to go to, instead of to Mum's to have a fight or to the basement of the building on Mass Avenue.

We had a very nice crossing, met up with some young people in Second Class and had a great time. Until I caught cold due to the very cold air-conditioning. Outside it was pretty hot, but inside it was too cold. I think I got it at the cinema, which was freezing. Luckily it was just before we reached Genoa, from whence we were driving along the Italian Riviera to Rome. I got steadily worse and in Rapallo we consulted a doctor and phoned Dr. Hufnagel. I had a light case of pleurisy, but it hurt horribly. I kept wanting to massage the place in my back where it was concentrated, and that was the worst thing to do. It lasted for about a week and then we drove to Rome, where I saw another doctor and was cured. The funny thing was that these doctors were so intimidated by my scar and the operation itself, that they asked me what I thought should be done and would not hazard a treatment independently.

Ulvia left us in Rome and flew back to Cairo. We stayed on for another month or so and saw all our usual friends, the Portanovas, the Boideffs, Moritz of Hesse, Harry Cushing, Hassan Momtaz who had married his French girlfriend by then.

To my surprise and Salah's horror, he received a wire from Fawkia, saying that their sister Leila was arriving in Rome with Ibrahim, Fawkia's husband, for urgent medical treatment. Leila was duly hospitalised and Ibrahim joined us in our activities. Salah could still not stand him and one evening, Ibrahim outdid himself in his tactless way. I had been looking at my passport and noticed that the new government had not had time to produce new passports and this one had the royal arms rather inadequately covered by the new stamp. Ibrahim said it was a good thing that Egypt was no longer a kingdom and that the King had abdicated. I turned on him like a fury, saying that I found him excessively rude and he had no right to insult my family. Salah was delighted, stopped the car and told him to get out. Next day, he apologised profusely, and rejoined our group.

Finally, we had to go home, this time on the Ausonia. We had a very agreeable trip and were on good terms.

Back in Cairo, we resumed the old life more or less. My marriage was going none too well, and Ulvia's was on the rocks. She had tasted too much freedom, she liked going out and had been drinking a lot. Shehriar hated nightclubs and drank very little, if at all. He liked to stay at home, have friends in, talk, gamble sometimes, and do nothing much. She was bored to tears by this life, started to rebel and go out by herself when her husband refused to go with her. He was also extremely jealous I found out later. The great love was over as far as she was concerned and he just could not live a life of drinking and confusion. I have always loved Shehriar dearly, like another brother and was very unhappy when they separated. What I do remember was our last dinner

Nevine, Said Chaarawi, Claire Bibaoui, Fawkia el Orabi

together at the Ermitage restaurant as couples, Salah and I, Ulvia and Shehriar. It was very pleasant, but changed nothing.

I was not doing much better. I did not have the same problems, rather the reverse. I was sick of going out every night with the same boring people. I was also getting sick of Salah. The horrendous jealousy had turned to indifference. Also I had another man in my sights. Salah, after years of pretending not to be jealous, suddenly began making scenes. The only thing I wanted was to get rid of him, but I did try to limp along and pretend.

Unfortunately, two events brought things to a head. Ulvia invited the other man and his wife to dinner at Schutz when Salah was there. When Salah saw him, he jumped out of our bedroom window into the garden and left. I was livid. Just the kind of thing to start a scandal. Daddy was furious with Ulvia, who had acted without thinking, or perhaps to please me.

Another time, we were at the bar of Montaza Palace, and I was listening to an old friend telling me about the death of his father. Salah started to make a fuss and we went home on bad terms. We were sitting in the kitchen at Schutz about to have a beer, when in came Daddy and Salah who had intended to spend the night there, was too embarrassed to do so and left. Daddy, instead of leaving quickly when he saw us together, stuck around probably thinking he could smooth things over if we were fighting.

We spent one last day together at Agami and were quite friendly, but I suppose it was too late by then. I could no longer stand the sight of Salah and in spite of Hussein Khairy's please, I insisted on divorcing him in September 1958. Hussein was the husband of my cousin, Princess Hadidja Hassan, and a friend of both Salah and me. Poor Hussein, he tried so hard. Salah offered me a trip to Europe, an emerald ring, even a child, but I was adamant. I realised, even as I was refusing to reconsider, that I might end by regretting my decision. I sometimes do regret it, and wonder what my life would have

Ulvia

been like if I'd remained with my husband. I honestly think that the relationship had rotted to the extent that we would never have been able to put it back together again. To become philosophical about it, I firmly believe that this is one instance when I definitely had a choice. God let me decide all by myself; my choice was not influenced by an extraneous event. It was a case of pure Free Will.

**

I have reached the end of the Golden Years. Now begin the supremely unwelcome Difficult Days. Difficult or not, you carry on somehow.

I would like to emphasise our great love for the Garden City house. My mother tried to recreate it in Washington D.C. at Mass Avenue with the most success as she had many of the bibelots and much of the furniture from Cairo. Every time one of us happened upon a place reminding us of Garden City, it was immediately communicated to the rest of our "private family." Sometimes it was only the height of a ceiling or the way the light filtered into a room through the slats of a half-lowered shutter, the graceful fall of a staircase in a hotel, the dimensions of a hall.

Daddy had Garden City photographed room by room before we left it at last, so reluctantly. It was a wrench like death. I dreamt of Garden City for years. In my dreams, it was all a great mistake and we were back home again. I could see my father's dressing room where we were summoned every day to say good morning to our parents. The violet flowers of the jacaranda tree outside his window danced in the gentle breeze and we could smell Daddy's talcum powder as he dressed, hidden behind the screen near the washbasin.

In the hall upstairs, the light came from the huge coloured-glass window which gave onto the garden and took up most of the wall. One small pane was always open in summer and through it shone the green lawn below.

Ali's room had an enormous balcony from which you could see the buildings which had housed the British HQ during the War. On the other side was the Ibrahimia School, which lots of our future male friends attended. They whistled and yelled at us whenever we appeared in the garden. Ali played football with Sambo's sons and as they needed more players, both Ulvia and I were roped in. I was always the goalkeeper, and a very good one too. Not much energy or running around was required and as the goal itself was quite narrow, my task was easy. Of course, this brought even louder shrieks from the Ibrahimia.

I remember *my* sitting room with the baby grand Bechstein and the bookcases filled with *my* books. I was allowed to close the doors and play away for as long as I wanted to. It was a refuge and who does not need a refuge at times?

During the difficult days of exile, one recalled the luminous, but soft light of Egypt. Not the eye-burning midday sun, a light in which you cannot see, which scorches your brain, leaves you incapable of movement. No, not that. The light so hard to describe. The incredible colours of a sunset across the Nile behind the Pyramids, or the blazing orb plunging into the Mediterranean in Alexandria. The golden pink touching the sand and the palms trees with glory as you sail down the Nile from Luxor to Aswan. The white light over a turquoise sea in Sidi Abdel Rahman and the brighter light shining and shining on the Red Sea.

Egypt to me is light, so indescribable, so many shades. You can never encompass all that beauty. The bad side makes no difference. It is logical. Everything has a bad side, even a very bad side. As you contemplate the dirt and squalor, suddenly the moon comes out, a huge white moon, and the ugliness is transformed into silver splendour. At dawn driving back from a hectic evening or just travelling early to the airport, again another light, soft and luminous at the same time, with a gossamer mist effacing the outlines of buildings. Then again at night crossing one of the Nile bridges, the lamps burn yellow, the river glistens and reflects the lights of moon and lamps, you see nothing but light and water. Then the eerie and beautiful sound of the Call to Prayer.

And so we emigrated to another life.

And we adapted.

Princess Nevine Halim is retired. She lives between Alexandria and Lausanne.